Ego Sum

Ego Sum

Corpus, Anima, Fabula

Jean-Luc Nancy

Translated and with an Introduction
by Marie-Eve Morin

FORDHAM UNIVERSITY PRESS

NEW YORK 2016

This book was originally published in French as Jean-Luc Nancy,
Ego Sum, Copyright © 1979 Flammarion, Paris.

Ouvrage publié avec le concours du Ministère français chargé
de la Culture–Centre National du Livre.

This work has been published with the assistance of the French
Ministry of Culture–National Center for the Book.

Fordham University Press has no responsibility for the persistence or accuracy of URLs for external or third-party Internet
websites referred to in this publication and does not guarantee
that any content on such websites is, or will remain, accurate or
appropriate.

Fordham University Press also publishes its books in a variety of
electronic formats. Some content that appears in print may not
be available in electronic books.

Visit us online at www.fordhampress.com.

Library of Congress Cataloging-in-Publication Data available
online at catalog.loc.gov.

Printed in the United States of America

18 17 16   5 4 3 2 1

First edition

CONTENTS

Jean-Luc Nancy

For Marie-Eve

Of this book written thirty-five years ago, will I dare say that it has not lost any of its freshness for me? I will, provided of course that I do not read it again. Were I to read it now, I would undoubtedly find it flawed in many ways and marked by the time of its writing. But first, I avoid as much as possible—interpret this any way you want—rereading my own texts. And second, in the case of this particular book, I am freed from the obligation and the care of rereading it in a more specific way, since it has never ceased reworking, repeating, and renewing itself within me— somewhere in an obscure region I have neither the desire nor perhaps even more the time to explore for new material to write about but where at the same time I know that the book still resonates, always producing new scions.

Ego sum. Today, I would only have to add an exclamation mark. "Ego sum!" Yes, of course, I am! Of course, this does not mean anything—that's evident, it is evidence itself. There is nothing to add: I am, and I am saying it. I say that I am, and that's the same thing as being—for a speaking being at least. And if the meaning of being of such a being is found nowhere else than in the verb "being" understood in a transitive way, which discredits both the intransitive verb (Hegel's "spiritless copula") as well as the substantive (Heidegger's "Being that is not"), if, in other words, the human *Dasein* *is* in that it transitively exists its own being, this transitivity is only given in saying or speaking [*le dire*].

If "being" names—in an unnamable way—the act whereby existence finds itself existing (received within the totality of beings, collected and thrown at the same time, ex-posed), then "speaking" names, for the speaking-existent, the act whereby this existent is ex-posed and the mode of this exposition. This mode consists in nothing other than the fact of "saying Being," which is as well its saying-being: it *is*—exists—insofar as it says that it is.

What is that to say? Perhaps nothing other than the following: It is as language that there is "being"—and this is why there is no "Being," but only the saying "being" (or in other words the tautology: "beings are"), that is, the act whereby the existent ex-ists, or, finally, makes sense. "Sense" entails a sending or a referral to another, be it the same addressed or envisaged as other.

Is Descartes not manifestly *other* when he declares "*I am*"?

So much so that it suffices to extrapolate from Heidegger to join up with Descartes on the opposite side of what Heidegger thought he had to designate under his name, that is, "the *subjectum* . . . misinterpreted as an individual present-at-hand I-thing [*vereinzelten vorhandenen Ichding*]."[1] Of course, it is from Heidegger on that this rereading is possible. However, this does not mean that this reading would only consist in a fantastic overinterpretation; rather, it means that both resources are present together in Descartes, as every great philosophy both hides and reveals the double possibility of an enclosure and a disenclosure. At the same time, *I am* posits (itself as) an *Ichding* and exposes (itself as) being-saying. This double valence is very well measured by the fact that Heidegger, in forging the word *Ichding*, does not pay attention to the fact that the German *Ich* (as well as the English *I*) does not permit differentiating between "I" and "me" as clearly as the French. For if the German language has at its disposal the objective cases *mich* and *mir*, *Ich* (written with a majuscule, like a noun) can be used to say either "I" or "me." "*Das Ich*" with Freud denotes what is translated in French as "*le Moi*," literally "the Me."[2] We can of course say "*le Je*" in French (as we say "the I" in English), but it is not part of common usage since "*je*" retains in French the exclusive value of a *shifter*;[3] it sets the utterance in motion within the statement. It cannot, or only with difficulty, pass into the position—in the strong sense of the term—of a substance, and hence of a substantive.

2

It was therefore necessary to come to understand that the thinking substance is only substance insofar as one can recognize it as having various attributions: doubting, affirming, negating, knowing, willing, imagining, sensing (without forgetting loving and hating, which appear in the French text of the *Meditations*).[4] But these attributions are not attributes of a *subjectum* or of a *suppositum*. They consist in the actions of an *I*, actions that only act insofar as *I* . . . doubt, for example, and then affirm, and so forth. *I* does not subsist independently of these actions, and if it affirms that it *is*, this means that its being is indubitably included in each of these actions as its agent. Yet, the agent is not the acting subject: it is the acting insofar as it acts. "Doubting" is impossible unless an "I" doubts. But "I" is impossible if not in the act of doubting, affirming, loving, and so forth.

In this way, the sense of "being" [*sens d'"être"*] ought not to be understood as a "sense of Being" [*"sens de l'Être"*]. But the sense of "being" is the act of speech, which acts within all of the mentioned attributions, for even when I simply sense without saying anything, the "I" of the "I sense" is pronounced silently as the knowing-oneself-sensing (or sensing-oneself-sensing) of the existent that senses, and thus senses *itself*.

At this point, it becomes impossible not to consider the "I" of every sensing existence, hence of plant and animal existence—at the very least, and without excluding a more extensive reflection on the mineral as exposed to actions outside and within itself. Of course, at this point we depart resolutely from Descartes and from Heidegger, but it is by plying the oars that they together have given us. One will add that if every existence is exposed—insofar as it is plural/singular—this exposition is always and everywhere mutual, according to regimes that remain admittedly diverse, but thanks to which a sense circulates, the sense of the world, a sense that is thus "one" only insofar as it concerns one world, but that is nonetheless heterogeneous in itself and disseminated as are the five senses, the three kingdoms of nature (to which one should add the technical kingdom), or the thousands of spoken languages.

The "I" exists only when it is articulated, and hence seems to be the pre-rogative of the speaking animal. But what this "I" gives us to understand at the same time as its being-saying is that this "being"—this speaking to one-self/one another that comes down to a making sense for oneself/one another (and not simply to a "making sense")—applies, through the mouth of the human being, to the totality of what exists. The sense of being-saying is not a sense imputed by the human being to the other beings that are inca-pable of expressing themselves. It is the sense that is said from all beings to all others through the speech that is not so much reserved for one of these beings than carried by this one being for the sake of all, in the same way in which mineral concretion is carried by another being, or colored profusion, sonorous emotion, etc. The becoming-technical of the world, the metamor-phoses of life, of species, of relations throughout the universe, of energy, all participate in this being-saying since technique is pure sense—referral from one instance to another (for example, of heat to pressure and movement, of movement to production and transportation, etc.)—while language, for its part, is really the first technical qualification of the speaking existent.

At this point it is understood that one does not leave Descartes behind, for whom "I am" provides the matricial evidence of a knowledge that is math-ematical because calculability is necessary to a mastery that is oriented by human ends and diverted from the adventurous meditation on divine ends. The fact that technology, today, uncovers a proliferation of ends, ends that become one after the other means for new ends that are themselves always more and more distant from any finality, this fact takes us beyond Descartes and Heidegger—but toward more "I am," so to speak, toward a more pointed sense of what "being-saying" means, or toward the in principle unfinish-able sense of the existence of the world.

3

"Through the mouth of the human being," I said. Since I wrote this book, the mouth is the other motif that never leaves me, even if I have not written much more about it, as if I was waiting (but who, "I"?) for a special occa-sion, the sudden discovery of the opportunity for an epic of the mouth.

The mouth: through which breath flows, and with breath sound, and within sound the immaterial sense finely woven in the phonemes, in their resonances, their harmonics, and their background noise. The mouth: through which food is absorbed, the digestion of which metabolizes energies in the delicate arrangement of muscular, nervous, and hormonal capacities giving rise to gestures, actions, passions, and the words that accompany, follow, or precede them. The mouth: through which emerges one of the major openings of the body, a body that exists only by being exposed from top to bottom and all the way through to influxes, affluxes, and refluxes of its near and far extremities, as well as of its entrails, always caught up, again and again, in the pushes and repulsions of the agitated masses among which it is thrown. The mouth: this jetty that says "I," sometimes shouting it and at other times stifling it.

The mouth: the orifice the elastic pulped edge of which draws the mobile contours of the opening of a sense that is each time other, singular, thrown and suspended in various ways, interrupted, without accomplishment, so that it can better retain in suspense the force of its impulse.

From the representation of a "me" posited in front of itself and thus "encapsulated" in itself, as Heidegger sometimes says,[5] but without destroying this representation (since we know far too well the considerable risks connected with this subobjectity), we attempt to pass, slowly, gently, almost insidiously, to this other thought that is not a representation but the experience of the mouth: speech, address, and why not song, and kiss?

4

A further comment, on the surprise.

Undoubtedly, a great philosopher, like a great artist, cannot but traverse the centuries and the continents unscathed. Anaximander, Wu Daozi, and King David testify to this fact. Besides, Descartes was convinced—or feigned to be convinced—that the Ancients had possessed and hidden a truth and that it was incumbent upon him to bring it to light once again. But Descartes himself traverses space-time at a singular and surprising speed. His name, his portrait, the phrase *cogito ergo sum* cling to the whole of our philosophical memory as a kind of emblem to which only a few are equal. There is something striking, decisive, and luminous (blinding even) about this emblem, which makes of it both a banner and a prerequisite for thought.

But the most important moment in Descartes is less this *cogito, ergo . . .* , which appears as a deduction, than the nondeduced *ego sum*. The latter no doubt includes the *cogitatio* that led to it. Yet, the second *Meditation* has less to do with the appearance of a deduction than with the performance of a leap: I doubt, and this doubt suddenly springs forth as indubitable, absolutely certain: "I am." We can take the "therefore" as being already included in the utterance, but, precisely, it remains at this exact moment enveloped and is not declared explicitly since the certainty springs forth from a piece of evidence more than from a conclusion.

I am surprises itself. We were not expecting it. We were busy calling everything into doubt, uncompromisingly. Nothing was secure from this doubt. Suddenly, this very gesture of putting aside or in brackets is acknowledged in its certainty, that is, in its own peculiar evidence. One cannot doubt this gesture, that is, call me into doubt.

Or rather: I cannot call myself, the *ego* that utters these words, into doubt, and not a "me" that would supposedly be the reference of this subject. The I is not a referent but only a speaker, who says "I." It says "I am" and it tautologizes its "I" since the Latin verb *sum* already contains the first person pronoun and has no need of *ego*. I am and I am only that which says "I am." I am the one who says "I am." Unshakable certainty—and complete surprise with regard to the doubt that we have just passed through and that spread before our eyes with obstinacy.

I am—yes, this is certain. But this surprises me in my search for something secure since I have consciously established that nothing is secure. Nothing is known for sure, nothing is secured as object of a certain knowledge. Surprise! I, who doubts, am, and that is not in doubt.

I do not know who or what or which one I am. That will be discovered later. But I am. I am my own surprise. Of course, this surprise includes my thought, my *cogitatio*. But this *cogitation* remains enveloped as such. It does not yet know itself for what it is: it receives itself as its own surprise.

This surprise, this character of surprise that Descartes contrives so well in the text of the second *Meditation*, this irruption of evidence that proceeds not from an argument but from a form of experience, has undoubtedly played a determining role in unleashing the force that imprints these words into the history of thought. *Ego sum* erupts like a flash. It takes the place of Parmenides's "It is," the subject of which was Being itself, then barely a subject but rather the "to be" taking hold of its being apart from any other being.

It is (Parmenides), I am—first two surprises. The third one will be "we exist" (Hegel, Heidegger)—a surprise that will carry the "I" outside of the utterance (since no one can say "we" without supposing endless complicated operations) and will also carry "Being" outside of subsistence up to the nothing or the opening of the *ex*—that is, of a properly infinite outside.

If there is a surprise, it means that something or someone was hidden. Indeed, ego *sum* lifts a mask, or many masks. The masks of "Monsieur Descartes" or of "Polybius, the Mathematician"; the mask of a heroic knight or that of a good Christian son of God; even the mask of the King's loyal subject since his texts are published abroad. But above all the mask of a *cogito* that would form, all by itself, a thinking substance completely detached from the extended substance and floating above it. For the crux of the issue is to grasp both substances as united into an indivisible, indissociable *unum quid* who goes about his business as engineer, traveler, physician, gentleman and philosopher. He goes about his business—what a surprise!—like everybody and anybody. *Anyone, anybody.* Already outside, then, already surprised by the bustle of the great world outside.

—July 2014

Ego Sum opens with a reflection on *l'actualité*, the news or the current situation, and on the relation between philosophy and this *actualité*. Though the book was written in the late 1970s, the issue that is at the core of Nancy's reflection on Descartes, namely the problematic return of the Subject, remains very much our own today. *Ego Sum*, then, is not only important for readers of Nancy's work who would like to trace the development of his thought, but it also provides us with an essential reflection of the constitution of the Subject. What *Ego Sum* teaches us is that we should not be too hasty in declaring the death of Subject, since this death might well be, as Derrida would say, its most effective way of living on. The living death of the Subject in postmodernity might well already be inscribed in its Cartesian birth so that all our deconstructions of the subject would remain more indebted to Descartes than we would admit.

The current situation, as it is described by Nancy in the opening pages of *Ego Sum*, is one where the "deconstruction" of the Subject is in full swing—one could even say that it has become fashionable. One speaks of the Subject as an effect (of the text, of history, of power, and so forth) and believes that one has overcome the metaphysics of the Subject and left Descartes behind. Indeed, the Cartesian Cogito was (at least if we follow the Heideggerian interpretation) the moment of the self-grounding and self-positing of the subject of thought and knowledge. For Heidegger, this is the inaugural moment of modern metaphysics, where the "I" becomes the *subjectum*, the underlying subject of representation, which is absolutely certain of itself. At this point, certainty becomes the measure of truth and truth becomes the adequation between representations within the subject and objects that stand before it. Such a Cartesian conception of the Subject is already disrupted, "deconstructed," by the discourse of psychoanalysis, and especially that of Lacanian psychoanalysis. Yet, as Nancy has shown in *Le titre de la lettre*, his first book, published in 1973 and written with his colleague and longtime friend Philippe Lacoue-Labarthe, the Lacanian discourse inadvertently reconstitutes the Subject it sought to disrupt and overcome. Lacan does show that the "Subject" is not the Cartesian subject conscious of itself and transparent to itself in all its utterances: The gap that is opened between the subject of the statement (the "shifter") and the subject who speaks or utters the statement leads to the impossibility for the subject of identifying himself with himself without detour (through language). The speaking subject is in fact a spoken subject, the locus of the signifier and not the master of meaning. What Nancy and Lacoue-Labarthe show, however, is that, despite all displacements, Lacanian psychoanalysis still presupposes the value of subjectivity and develops a theory of the subject (albeit a negative theory of a split subject). The lack or gap at the heart of the subject becomes the foundation of a subject certain of itself as noncoincidence,[1] and psychoanalysis becomes the scientific discourse that masters this subject. In *Ego Sum*, Nancy reasserts this position toward both traditional and contemporary psychoanalysis: "at the moment when the philosophical question of the ineffectivity of the subject *comes about*, what is called 'psychoanalysis' only unsettles the anthropological regime by obstinately reinvesting the position of a discourse of the subject, according to both possibilities of this genitive." While psychoanalysis problematizes the Cartesian subject, it does nothing to undermine "the *imperium* of the subject."

Such a reconstitution of the Subject is not, however, exclusive to psychoanalysis. As Nancy writes:

> From all sides, then, whether as the unconscious, or as history, language, machine, text, body, or desire (and everywhere where the subject is declared to be simple effect-of-subject), these new subjects have so far only produced the aggravation, or in a simpler and more massive way, the exacerbation of the *status* of the Subject: the consolidation of the *substratum* as such, which *substrates itself*, if one may say so, all the more and all the better now that it

claims to sink deeper outside of the figure of the conscious subject, of the subject as creator or as master.

This is perhaps even true of Heidegger, whose discourse presents us with "a subject-who-knows-what-is-happening-with-the-subject-of-representation, who knows how to represent it as the illusion of the presence-to-self of a consciousness, or as the subject of a phantasm, and who thus knows how to represent himself, that is, to present to himself the truth about Descartes as thinker of an illusory or phantasmatic subject-of-representation." It is also true of Foucault's reading of madness in Descartes. As Derrida points out in "*Le cogito ou l'histoire de la folie*,"

> Foucault wanted madness to be the *subject* of his book in every sense of the word: its theme and its first-person narrator, its author, madness speaking about itself. Foucault wanted to write a history of madness *itself*, that is madness speaking on the basis of its own experience and under its own authority, and not a history of madness described from within the language of reason, the language of psychiatry *on* madness.[2]

The first question, then, is: In what language can the mad speak about his or her madness? If *logos* or reason is to be excluded from the discourse on madness, then only a mad discourse could be adequate to madness. While Foucault, according to Derrida, acknowledges these difficulties, he still attempts to write the archaeology of the silence that surrounds madness. For Foucault, this silence is a historical fact: The mad were excluded and silenced, and it is this exclusion that forms the presupposition of Descartes's discourse and of classical reason. Foucault's discourse will let this silence speak. Yet, just as psychoanalysis becomes the theory of the split subject (or of the psychotic subject), Foucault's archeology produces the discourse of the mad subject and hence puts itself in the position of the master of meaning, the producer of signification it sought to unsettle.

The lesson is that any theoretical discourse, no matter how subversive, always produces a subject: the subject of the discourse (in both senses of the genitive). Put differently, no matter how split or mad the subject of discourse is, this discourse on such a subject itself presupposes a master subject, a subject who is certain of himself and is the master of the meaning of this split or mad subject. As Nancy puts it: "Theory—that is, the Subject." It is in this context that the necessity of a detour through Descartes makes itself felt for Nancy. Why? Because the collapse of the Subject, or rather the collapse of its substance, is already inscribed in its Cartesian inauguration. Already in Descartes, the Subject does not stand firm and needs to be propped up. This means, then, that far from overcoming Descartes or leaving him behind, contemporary discourses that disrupt the Subject as self-conscious, transparent, and certain of itself, and uncover its madness or split, only exhaust the essential possibilities found in Descartes's discourse itself.

At the same time, by following Descartes's writings, by following the twists and turns by means of which Descartes attempts to make the subject (or make himself as the subject of his own discourse) visible, Nancy's goal is to reach "the place, indeed [to go] back to the instant of a foundation, that of the Subject—in order to lend an ear to what only the foundation can make audible, because it triggers it and brings it about: the whisper of the subject that utters itself there, and collapses there." Nancy's wager is that it is at the moment of the foundation of modern subjectivity, a foundation which always already includes all the possibilities of its exhaustion, that another thought of "the subject" is possible. This "subject" speaks but he is not the speaking subject or the subject of the utterance; he is not even the neuter, impersonal *ça* of *ça parle*; this "subject" is *ego* (not *the* ego), a mouth that opens and says, in turn: *dum scribo, larvatus pro Deo, mundus est fabula, unum quid*.

As should be clear by now, there is much overlap between the concerns of *Ego Sum* and Nancy's early works. Both the question of the Subject, which was central to *The Title of the Letter*, as well as the question of the mode of presentation of philosophical discourse and of the relation between literature (style, fashion) and system (concept, system), which were at the core of Nancy's discussion of Kant in *Logodaedalus* and Hegel in *The Speculative Remark*, find their way in *Ego sum*. Yet, *Ego Sum* occupies somewhat of a unique place in Nancy's early works. The French editor calls it "a detour," albeit a motivated one. It is true that Nancy has returned to Kant and to Hegel many times, and even to Lacan, but his interest in Descartes seemed to have remained limited (except for the very short text "The Extension of the Soul").

At the same time, as Nancy indicates in the preface to this English translation, *Ego Sum* continues to influence his thinking, themes from this book reappear again and again in his later work: the mouth, the body, the extension of the soul. It would not be an exaggeration to claim that the meditations on the body Nancy undertakes in *Corpus* are made possible by the thinking of *ego* as *unum quid* and as the union of the soul and the body undertaken in *Ego Sum*. Freud's famous posthumous note, "Psyche is extended, knows nothing about it," to which Nancy returns in almost all his writings on the body, appears here for the first, in a meditation on the mouth. This mouth is also related to two other concepts that will play an important role in Nancy's later thought: spacing (which here translates Heidegger's *räumen*) and areality. Interestingly, a few years after the publication of *Ego Sum* and before coming back to the areality of the body (both in the sense of its nature of an area or surface and of a slight, faint, suspended reality), Nancy will use the logic of arealization to describe the "being" of the community.[3]

Another important theme that finds its premise in *Ego Sum* is that of exposition. In his later works, exposition will become the basic ontological category of Nancy's thinking: Being is exposition; to be is to be exposed to (oneself and others) so that there is no inside that would preexist the moment of exposition. One exists as exposed upon a limit that opens one to an exteriority, which means that such exteriority and such movement of opening unto is an essential moment of existence that prevents any closing up or immanence of any existent. In *Ego Sum*, the category of exposition appears in a discussion of the mode of presentation of Descartes's discourse. Nancy focuses, in *"Larvatus pro Deo"* and *"Mundus Est Fabula,"* on the masks and portraits Descartes uses to present himself (and his Method) to the reader/viewer. Far from being mere literary ornaments, these devices, and the fictive viewer or readers they entail, are necessary to the Subject's being and truth. As a result, exposition unsettles the distinction between interiority and exteriority and forms the basis of Nancy's reading of the cogito in *"Unum Quid."* If ego exists only in its uttering "ego," then there can be no pure self-apprehension of thought by itself. At the same time, by emphasizing the movement of withdrawal or distinction that is concomitant to the expression of ego, Nancy makes clear that exposition is not a melting or blending together. It is such double movement of contact/separation or entanglement/disentanglement that will form the basis of Nancy's think-ing of singularity.[4] The portrait as the presentation of the subject, its expo-sition and withdrawal, its exhibition and intimacy, has also become an important theme in Nancy's writings on art.[5]

Another theme that has resurfaced in recent years is that of frankness. Indeed, in his short book *Identity: Fragments, Frankness*, Nancy returns to the thought of the *I am* as frankness, calling the "I am," *ego sum*, a frank point, a point or place from which identity is uttered.[6] It is in his reading of Descartes, of the fable of frankness that is his *Discourse on the Method*, that Nancy uncovered this complex relation between the cogito (or the existence of ego) and frankness.

It is not my aim here to retrace the detail of Nancy's steps through Descartes's texts. Nancy is not proposing a series of arguments here; rather, he is guiding his reader through the meanders of Descartes's writings, pay-ing special attention to passages that are often dismissed by commentators as mere literary devices. The result is a provocative and unprecedented reading of Descartes, but one that can hardly be summarized and rather needs to be followed step by step by each reader.

My first concern in this translation has been to follow the flow of Nancy's French without hindering the readability of the English. I have tried to be as consistent as possible in my rendering of French words, but I have often departed from my chosen translation in favor of a more idiomatic (or plainer) English expression. I have done so when it appeared to me that a word was not used as a technical term. For example, *exposition*, which will become a major ontological category in Nancy's later work, is here not yet used as a technical term and so has been rendered as exhibition or exposition depend-ing on context. I have also tried to keep Nancy's somewhat idiosyncratic use of punctuation when it was essential to the rhythm of his prose and of his thinking.

I have, however, added bibliographical references to Descartes's oeuvre when these were missing in the original. (In "*Dum Scribo*" I have also added quotations marks around passages that were obviously quotes from Des-cartes but not indicated as such.) I have always provided references to the

English translations, using Cottingham, Stoothoff, and Murdoch's translation of *The Philosophical Writings of Descartes* published by Cambridge University Press, rather than keeping Nancy's references to Ferdinand Alquié's three-volume edition of Descartes's *Œuvres philosophiques* published by Garnier, but I have provided references to the Adam and Tannery (AT) edition as well. I have normally provided the AT reference to the Latin text, except when Nancy is explicitly referring to the French edition of the *Meditations* or the *Principles*. This should allow English readers to consult easily both the translated text and the original.

A major challenge of this translation was navigating between Descartes's Latin, the French translation of Descartes (which Nancy often relies upon), Nancy's paraphrases of Descartes, and the standard English translation of Descartes. For the French reader of *Ego Sum*, many of the phrases used by Nancy, without quoting Descartes directly, will nevertheless resonate with Descartes's original. For this reason, I have tried to stick as close as possible to the standard English translation of Descartes's text, rather than merely translating Nancy's words, though this was often not possible. For example, Nancy quotes the passage at the beginning of the *Discourse* where Descartes states that he is "presenting this work as a story." The French word he uses is *proposer*. Later in the chapter, Nancy will often return to this *proposition* of the *Discourse*. Here he does not mean the statement (or proposition) we find in the Discourse but instead the fact that the Discourse is presented or proposed as a fable. Instead of sticking with the English translation "presentation," which was already used for *présentation*, I have switched to proposal. Another example: the famous *quoties a me profertur* of the second *Meditation* is rendered in French as "*chaque fois que je la prononce*" but in English as "each time it is put forward by me." While the Latin *profertiare*, which also gives us the French *proférer*, does not quite correspond to the English "to pronounce" and is much closer to the "put forward" chosen by the English translators, Nancy does go on to emphasize the sense of moving one's mouth and making sounds, which seem to be best rendered by "pronounce" than the "put forward" one finds in the English translation.

Of course, the best rendering for both *prononcer* and *proférer* might well have been simply "to utter," but I have decided to reserve utterance and uttering for *l'énonciation* and *l'énoncer* respectively, while I have rendered *l'énoncé* as statement. This was not an easy decision to make, and I am aware that it goes against at least some, if not most of the existing translations of Nancy. Indeed, in *The Title of the Letter*, Raffoul and Pettigrew use "statement" for *l'énoncé* but "enunciation" for *l'énonciation*. This follows the standard uses of these terms in Lacan scholarship, where one speaks of the distinction between the subject of the enunciation and the subject of the utterance (sometimes also called the subject of the enunciated). In an article on *Ego Sum* where he explicitly relates this text to the earlier book on Lacan, Ian James settles for "enunciation" and "enunciating," but often leaves the French untranslated.[7] In my own work on Nancy, I have followed James and used "enunciation" and "enunciating."[8] However, Christine Irizarry, in her translation of quotations from "*Unum quid*" in Derrida's *On Touching*, uses "enunciated utterance" or simply "utterance" for *l'énonciation* and "uttering" for *l'énoncer*, while she opts for "enunciated utterance" again to render *l'énoncé*.[9] Richard A. Rand, in his translation of *Corpus*, is far less systematic in how he renders these terms.[10] The verb *énoncer* in all its forms is often rendered as "to enunciate" but sometimes also as "to state" or "to declare." *L'énoncé* is rendered as "statement" but also once as "declaration" and as "what is declared." *L'énonciation* is rendered variably as "declaration," "enunciation," or "statement." For his part, Daniel Brewer, in his translation of "*Mundus est fabula*," used "utterance" for *l'énoncé* and "uttering" for *l'énoncer*, leaving *l'énonciation* untranslated.[11] Given the number of times the noun *l'énonciation* appears in the last chapter of the book, this solution was not optimal for my purpose. At the same time, given that the context here is not Lacan but the performative in linguistics, the use of utterance or statement seems preferable to enunciation.

While *proférer* merely means "to utter," I have rendered *profération* as proclamation to keep the connotation of speaking out loud while avoiding the repeated use of utterance. Irizarry uses "proffered utterance" in this case and Rand "proferring." Even if in early use the verbs "to profer" (from the Latin *proferre*, in French *proférer*, "to carry forward," "to pronounce," "to utter") and "to proffer" (from the Old French *proferir*, also *poroffrir* or *paroffrir*, "to bring forward" in the sense of "to offer" or "to propose") were used almost indistinguishably,[12] the semantic connection between "proffer" and *proférer* seem tenuous today. Indeed, *proférer* is mostly used in expressions such as *proférer des menaces*, which certainly does not entail any offer or proposal.

Another difficulty had to do with Nancy's uses of reflexive verbs: *se décider*, *se poser*, *s'installer*, *s'établir*, and so on. I have used the English reflexive when it seemed to me to be required by Nancy's emphasis on the *se*, but I have the passive voice when it did not affect the meaning and made the text easier to read. *Se retrancher* has often been rendered straightforwardly as "to withdraw" though the (slightly more awkward) reflexive "to withdraw oneself" was used when it seemed necessary to emphasize the reflexive object of this withdrawal. Finally, to render the ambiguous expression *faire voir quelqu'un*, I have opted for "to make someone see and be seen" when Nancy was explicitly playing on the double entendre. When there is no double entendre, however, the simpler "to make visible" is used.

La pointe, which means the tip or the point (of, say, a pen or sword), has been rendered variously as "the extreme point," "the outermost tip," or "the outer extremity," depending on context. While the corresponding English idiom is "the cutting edge," changing the image from tip to edge meant losing the sense of what is farthest or foremost.

The reader will also notice that I have sometimes used the masculine pronouns to refer to the subject. This is partly to avoid the confusion that arose in many instances from the use of "it" but also because in these instances the subject in question was not only the (masculine) subject of modern philosophy but also, first and foremost, Descartes himself. When speaking of the viewer of Descartes's portrait, I have followed Nancy's indication in a footnote of "*Larvatus pro Deo*" and used the feminine pronouns.

The middle three chapters, which had already appeared in shorter versions in English translations before the publication of the French book,[13] have all been translated anew here. I consulted Ian McLeod's and Daniel Brewer's translations and compared my own decisions to theirs only after I had finished the first draft of the translation. I sometimes found their choices of words or phrases more compelling than mine and decided to follow their lead. There are, however, significant differences between the two English versions. First, Nancy expanded the essays that were included in *Ego sum* in 1979, adding a paragraph or a footnote here and there, and significantly reworking the end of "*Mundus est fabula*." Second, because I decided to use existing English translations of Descartes's texts and other sources rather than translate all quotations myself, my translation choices were often affected by these existing translations. Finally, I also had to be more careful about the consistency of the translation across chapters. Translations that would have worked well in one chapter were sometimes rejected because they did not work for other chapters. For example, in light of the frequent recurrence of the term *énonciation* in the last chapter of the book, it did not seem wise to keep the word in French, as Daniel Brewer decided to in his translation of *"Mundus est fabula."*

I would like to thank Jean-Luc Nancy for his enthusiasm for this project. Without it, I would probably not have undertaken such a daunting task. I would like to thank Fordham University Press for its support, in particular the late Helen Tartar, who commissioned the project, and Thomas Lay, who saw it through. I would also like to thank the Department of Philosophy at the University of Alberta for their financial support. By providing me with research assistants, it has made some of the tedious work of tracking down quotes and references (a work made difficult by the occasional absence of clear references in the original) easier and allowed me to focus on the translation of the text itself. I am of course also extremely grateful to these research assistants themselves: Nika Pona, who tracked down all Descartes quotations in the Adam and Tannery edition as well as in the English translation, and Emine Hande Tuna, who tracked down English translations of all the other sources used by Nancy. I also thank Brian Stimpson for his help tracking down a passage from Valéry's *Cahiers*. Special thanks also go to Maxime Allard, O.P., and Christopher Sauder for the invitation to speak at the Dominican University College in Ottawa in December 2013 and for the translation workshop they organized after my presentation. Special thanks also to all the students who attended this workshop. It was a pleasure to discuss translation issues with so many bilingual philosophy students, and our discussion influenced many of the decisions I ended up making later on. I am especially thankful to Vladimir Dukic, who not only combed through the manuscript carefully for typographical errors, grammatical mistakes, and inconsistencies but also provided insightful comments and suggestions on the penultimate draft, which led to a much improved translation. Finally, special thanks go to Philip Armstrong, whose suggestions on the final draft greatly improve the readability of the translation. Of course, I take full responsibility for any mistranslations and remaining errors. This translation was supported by the Social Sciences and Humanities Research Council of Canada.

. . . denique statuendum sit hoc pronuntiatum, Ego sum, ego existo, quoties a me profertur, vel mente concipitur, necessario esse verum.

. . . finally one must rule, establish, decide, erect as a statue and ground as a statute the fact that this pronouncement, the utterance, this statement, *I am, I exist*, each time I proclaim, propose or pronounce it, each time I conceive it in my mind or each time it is conceived by my mind, is necessarily true.

—DESCARTES, *Second Meditation*

Ego Sum: Opening

I. Quoties a me profertur . . .

Coming back, one might say, from exile, having been eclipsed for some years—in the Structure, the Text, or the Process—the subject occupies contemporary discourses once again . . .

. . . If we begin here, it is because I want—and it is not the first time[1]—to mark the opening of this work with a certain relation to our current situation [*l'actualité*], even to what is fashionable. This relation should be explained once again, especially since the circumstances are no longer the same.

As regards philosophical discourse, the present conjuncture can be schematized by means of the following duality or duplicity: a forgetting and a return, firmly bound to each other, of something that we call "philosophy."

It is not my intention to analyze this conjuncture as such, according to the rules of its economy and the stakes of its politics. But it is scarcely possible, in these conditions, to open a philosophical discourse (or one that is presumed to be philosophical: This is presented as a "book on Descartes," but not as a book of history) without attempting to indicate what kind of "discourse" is in question here. In fact, this will be a first way in which we, in turn, speak again of the subject.

Indeed, on the one hand, we have reached the point today where we do not even suspect, or suspect very little, that there exist philosophical works and discourses that, *as such*, entertain determinate and operative relations with our current situation in all its extension, that is, with what would in this case be deemed "nonphilosophical." Everything happens, on the contrary, as if this actuality could only be pointed out and reached in the immediate form of the empirical object. Everywhere this kind of discourse—or more precisely of commentary [*propos*], which mixes in variable proportion documentation and analysis, one and the other taken from the vast field of our new *epistēmē*[2]—spreads under the guise of theoretical work. In other words, documentation and analysis are taken from the field of a general anthropology that, even though it has gained access to the manipulation of the symbolic and makes use of psychology, sociology, history, psychoanalysis, biology, poetics, thermodynamics, and even mathematics, all relieved of their old positivism, nevertheless avails itself of a positivity, albeit of the highly sophisticated positivity (the technological lexicon imposes itself here) of the subject of the commentary in question. For this commentary is of the subject, both in its object and in its subject. In other words, *it is not* a discourse about, and it is even less a question of, what for the moment and for lack of a better term I will call the *being* of such a subject.

Without offering the following lines as a guarantee, and without simply holding them for the truth, I will not shy away from recalling everything that was correct about the following text from 1929, written by Heidegger:

> the analytic of everydayness has the methodological intention from the first
> of not allowing the interpretation of the Dasein in human beings to enter the
> realm of an anthropological-psychological description of man's "experiences"

and "faculties." Anthropological-psychological knowledge is not thereby declared to be "false." It is necessary to show, however, that with all its correctness it is not sufficient to hold in view from the start and constantly the problem of Dasein's existence.[3]

From this first point of view, our current situation consists, and insists, in the prolix expansion of the anthropological subject—a necessary consequence, and indeed more than a consequence: it is the effectuation of a metaphysics of the Subject, but at the same time, the *forgetting* of the metaphysical origin [*provenance*] and nature of this subject, a forgetting, ignorance, or denegation of metaphysics (or ontotheology) that is perpetuated by this subject. In this respect, the most pressing task [*actuelle*] can only be the most philosophical: it consists in showing this effectuation as such, and correlatively—in the mode of a paradox that will only surprise those whose ability to forget has definitely engulfed everything—this task consists in showing the ineffectivity of this effectuation. In other words, the task is to show how the anthropological profusion of the subject covers over and muffles the question—that is, as we will see in what follows, the voice—of someone: this someone, neither a subject nor the Subject, will not be named, but this book would like to let it call itself: *ego*.

If such is our first philosophical relation to our current situation, one would be right to object that such a relation is constitutive, even generative, of the philosophical attitude at every moment of its history. Besides, other things being equal, this relation will be found very explicitly at the beginning of the discourses of Plato, Descartes, Kant, Hegel, and so on. And in their work, one would not fail to find that such a relation constantly denounces the ineffectivity of the epoch and of its *epistēmē*. Hence, this relation itself must be analyzed according to two aspects. According to the first, it consists in the relation of mastery, of the will to mastery from which the philosophical as such proceeds. Hence, as we have known since Hegel and since Bataille,[4] this is the *servile* relation of philosophy to its epoch. Or else it consists in the anthropological relation of philosophy to its epoch, to its *epistēmē*, and to philosophy itself. Nothing testifies better to the servile and anthropological nature of philosophy than this will to dominate anthropology itself (by means of condemnation, subsumption, reduction, or foundation). No philosophy can fully escape it, no more here than else-where, today no more than yesterday. It is philosophy as subject.

But there is a second aspect. Philosophy as subject is not the subject of philosophy.[5] At least their identity is not simple, and the latter is not a subject. It is not the subject of the servile subjection to actuality. It is—if it *is* in any way—this other relation (which can be designated *or not designated* as "philosophical") through which our current situation, at every time, is *in act*. That is, it is not content to be simply actual, present, and enclosed within its entelechy, but *acts* of itself because what is in question within it (an ac-tive, troubling, dispossessing question) is its very self, that is, its timeliness [*actualité*], which is also to say its lack thereof. Each time—each *epoch* or each actual suspension of time—is troubled by the question of the ineffectivity of time. This relation, which is no longer to our current situation but which is the relation of this actuality to what it does not actualize, is the philo-sophical relation (and this again, whatever name it may take). And this rela-tion is unavoidable—it is no less avoidable than history. It comes about, at each time, even if one does not want it to come about (and it is not always, far from it, the professional philosopher that brings it about). This relation is, or puts into act what, of each time, comes. For example: that today the revived ineffectivity of the subject has come about. Philosophy is not and can never be *what* comes, what occurs; but the fact that it comes about bears the name and takes the form, in the West, of the philosophical. Hence one must philosophize . . . (What drives me, here as elsewhere, or rather what obligates me is this strange imperative: "you must discourse."[6] What also drives me, then, is undoubtedly "the excessive desire for theoretical in-sights, the unsophisticated pedantry of which is preferable, of course, to the sovereign allure of their adulteration, which is almost completely prevalent today."[7]) And philosophizing requires that one confronts relentlessly, by means of what comes about, what has come and has actualized itself within philosophy—for example, metaphysical anthropology.

> Our epoch . . . needs to work *tirelessly* to define metaphysics and free itself
> from it. It would indeed be catastrophic if *we* left the relation of the future
> world history (in part occurring, in part yet to come, always *also* ready to
> "not being able to take place") to its metaphysical past, in the same obscurity
> in which Marx left his relation to Hegel. Where would we then gather the

strength to denounce and prevent (by means of a kind of stylistic initiative, which is our only weapon) the return, under an appeal to socialism, of various barely rejuvenated Marxist "koinē," under the doctrinal cloak of which the historical powerlessness of what reigns today as "capitalism" would be perpetuated.[8]

To that I would only add that it is henceforth the return of all kinds of other "koinē"—non-Marxist, anti-Marxist—that must be challenged. All these "koinē" are anthropological, whether they appeal to history or to subjectivity.

And then we find, within our conjuncture, the other side of the duplicity— the complicit return of forgetting. This is the recent motif, noisy but in truth discreet at the same time, almost fleeting, of a new philosophy— so that we do not know if it has already had its day or if it is propagating itself imperceptibly—by which one essentially means (since we are not speaking here of the theses of this "philosophy," which are incidentally various and confused, but of the idea of philosophy they imply) philosophy as novelty. One has started, here and there, to name "philosophy" not the work of what is inactual or untimely [*l'inactuel*] but the heralding of an unheard-of actuality that is simply discontinuous with a whole past, itself decreed to be simply past, null and void, a past of false or bad prophets. This is the case because philosophy as novelty becomes, in both the strict and the vague sense, itself prophecy: It speaks-in-the-name-of, and it makes pompous predictions. In whose name? As if by chance, in the name of the same subject, the anthropological subject, who becomes, in the prophecy itself and so that there can be prophecy, a moral or moralizing subject. This "philosophy," which can only claim to be "new" because around it (and within it) one has forgotten what philosophy is about, consists in the decla- ration of the rights and desires of the subject. But, once again, it is not the content that matters here but the prophetic form. While making the subject speak, believing it can grasp or have a hold on the living flesh of its speech, the scream of its suffering or the song of its liberty (why then is this dis- course so pathetic?), this new "philosophy" does not worry about the inef- fectivity of this subject (and its metaphysical origin). It does not worry about what has now come about in philosophy—in the West—and keeps coming: namely, the end of the epoch where philosophy could be, or at least appear as, the vision (conception) of a world and of a history, and the prophetic heralding of this vision. To change conceptions, for example by substituting the ethical for the political, or the aesthetic for the historical, and so on, is to remain subjected to the regime of *the* conception in general: at the very moment when what is coming (to us) first announces itself precisely as the end of conception, or of the conceivability of conception. Those who "philosophize" without seeking to think this (obscure and, to say the least, ambiguous) end resemble those Romans of the dying Empire who sought to restore ancient cults, or to make up new ones. They do not suspect that the subject they are making speak—the subject of a conception of the world—might not henceforth be saying anything, whatever they might make it say. At the very least one should know what speaking means— and first of all when what is said is: *ego*.

A question of actuality and a pressing question for our time [*Question d'actualité*], then, if there is one.

WHERE THE SUBJECT SPEAKS AGAIN OF ITSELF

As with others, this actuality of the subject is not as new as it appears. Rather, it endows with the rather thin novelty of its anthropological and/or prophetic tone a motif of the subject that makes up the leitmotiv—in the strong sense of the word, the guiding motif—of Lacan's psychoanalysis. So it is a question of a motif that has persisted for no less than forty years in this "modern" form.[9] This should be recalled as much to give credit where credit is due, as to underline the continuity of an *imperium* of the subject through the most advanced of its nonphilosophical problematics.

To be fairer and more precise, one should say, rather: psychoanalysis— Freud's and Lacan's—will have constituted the furthest advance of the metaphysical problematic of the Subject. Simultaneously, it will have con- stituted the extreme anthropologization (as well as the socioinstitutional inscription of this anthropologism), *and*, as it often happens at any extreme point, it will have brought to light the limit of anthropology's critical fal- tering. This double process can be deciphered more and more clearly in the recent history of psychoanalysis; and whatever aspect of this history one might consider, it always relates in the final analysis to the question of the subject. The motif, introduced long ago by Lacan, of the subject of the utterance has finally given psychoanalysis the obligation and the means to assume a critical posture precisely toward that from which it believed to have been able to borrow this subject: linguistics.[10] The observation to be drawn here—namely, that linguistics cannot at bottom even reach the subject of the utterance—in reality (or if one prefers, in potentiality) bears upon the whole of anthropology; it was not by chance that the latter had for so long taken linguistics as its paradigm, at least in cases where it had not simply functioned as a motley inventory of technologies and enthnologies.

In that case, psychoanalysis might have carried out the philosophical task—and philosophy, in that actuality, would only play this other role, for which it is also well known, of a Don Quixote busy attacking the rear guards of science . . . This is not the case, however, and for a very simple reason. It has nothing to do with divisions, even less with oppositions or rivalries between "disciplines," and it does not exempt us from acknowledging all the ways in which the philosopher is actually indebted toward the psychoanalyst. The reason is the following: at the moment when the philosophical question of the ineffectivity of the subject *comes about*, what is called "psychoanalysis" only unsettles the anthropological regime by obstinately reinvesting the position of a discourse of the subject, according to both possibilities of this genitive. This is even, no doubt, the position Lacan attempted to assume up to the end, that is, up to an extremity that he never reached but always reaffirmed as the *telos* of his discourse. In the wake of Lacan—but maybe in any psychoanalytic wake *as such*—the most demanding attempts cannot but be renewed according to the same teleology.

Let us take the example of an especially revealing attempt, revealing because it aims, after Lacan and others but with a particular claim to its own radicality, to deconstitute the subject (the full subject, the master-subject) of analytical discourse.[11] In this way, by means of analysis, it seeks to cross an "epistemological break" that implies taking into account the constitutive gap between the "real of [the subject's] act" (which "reduces analysis to the zero-degree of signifying practices") and its "mathemic" or "discursive consistency," which would consist precisely not in the foundation or legitimation of this "real" but in the "rational" management of this very gap and of the "unobtainable and undecidable apodicticity" upon which it depends

(Petitot-Cocorda's text is about the "apodicticity" of psychosis, the unascribable psychotic subject of analysis). It is quite clear that, in spite of itself, such a claim (the epistemological version, in the end, of the Lacanian *Witz*) can only end up turning away from the very fact it wants to address, or wants the theory to take on: namely, the gap between the "real" and "discourse," for the theory that pretends, as such, to plunge into this gap is inevitably led to posit itself as the identification (the reduction) of this gap (or *as its subject*). (A result that is even more staggering since in psychoanalysis maybe more—or more visibly—than anywhere else "the real of [the subject's] act" coincides with the establishment of his discourse . . . But it is *also* this singular identity that the theory thus keeps itself from theorizing.)

Theory—that is, the subject—has always consisted in positing itself as the thought of the open abyss between the act of thinking and the discourse of thinking. As we will have occasion to review here, nothing else supports the nondiscursive operation of the Cartesian *cogito* (and it is no coincidence that this cogito is being reworked in the text I have just mentioned, as well as in many other analytical works,[12] here again according to a tradition that comes from Lacan). The theoretical operation has always properly consisted in the self-position, not of an immediate and naïve (or native) "knowledge," as a simplistic schematization of metaphysics might lead us to believe, but of the abyss between the thing and knowledge; this operation has even consisted, since Descartes at least, in the self-position and the self-foundation of the abyss between the thing of knowledge and the knowledge of that thing. This self-foundation of the abyss, this manner of exacerbating the abyss while at the same filling it, is the Subject's operation par excellence. The Subject's discourse can fold this self-foundation upon itself or unfold it as much as one wants. Each of these gestures is part and parcel of the theoretical program and reinforces the Subject, be it only its lack-to-itself.

Assuredly, no discourse can escape this. So it is only a matter of showing the following: psychoanalysis will in turn have accomplished this law of discourse and will have thereby given another—irreplaceable—twist to the completion of metaphysics, by exhibiting in the end the bare figure of "science," which has no other "object" than the law of its own discourse. The Subject hears itself there, and makes itself heard, infinitely.[13]

What is it still about, then? What could there be left? And what do we want here with our "philosophy"?

In effect, there is nothing left. The only thing left is what remains, the obstinate metaphysical reconstruction of analytical discourse, and of any discourse, or maybe even of an equivalence that would have slowly and silently been established between discourse and analysis, and which an acute observer could discover as the ground—the ineffective effectivity—of our current situation.

But this remains, precisely.[14] It stays in place (where else could it stay?). This place is therefore the one from which the Subject makes itself heard, and from which we nevertheless know that it might not give anything more to understand. Everything plays itself out in the *same* place, insofar as it is the place of the Same, the very place of the Same. This place could be said to be that of an "undecidable apodicticity"—it could, if it were not exactly *here* that everything must be decided. The undecidable is apodictic, or it turns into an apodicticity, only on the condition that one has first decided to take it and posit it, however undecidable it is, *as such*, and thus endow it with the strange *identity* of its undecidability, that is, to constitute it truly as substance or as Subject. Such is undoubtedly the ultimate turn taken by the discourse of the Subject in and thanks to analysis: The undecidable *taken as such* constitutes the most advanced decision (and the most secluded, sheltered decision, beyond the reach of discursive masteries, and for this reason so imperious) by means of which a discourse is given consistency, substance, and the stature of a Subject.[15]

Yet, one must nevertheless decide (but it is not a decision anymore, since it is necessary; and yet it is one, one that each subject of a discourse incessantly adopts or rejects) *not* to take as such what has no "as" and no "such" but is only undecided. The decided discourse of this indecision, the discourse of something that, undeciding itself, comes about, is the discourse of philosophy, of philosophy or of "what we still call by this name and has perhaps always disappeared," as Blanchot writes,[16] explaining further: "Philosophical discourse is first of all *without rights*. It says everything and could say everything, but it does not have the power to say it: it is a possible without power."[17]

It is not a matter of another discourse, even less of a discourse of the Other. It is not even a matter of this discourse that is here visibly held (printed) in the name of and under the title of "philosophy," but of what holds itself "behind what is said," to continue to recite Blanchot. It is a matter of "this *dis-course* precisely without rights, without signs, illegitimate, out of place, of ill omen, and for this reason, obscene, and always disappointing and in rupture, and at the same time, passing beyond any interdiction, the most transgressive, closest to the intransgressible Outside."[18]

What lets itself be heard in this way is "the obscure and disgusting whisper that the pure-impure philosophical speech would be."[19] This whisper is that of someone, a subject perhaps, but a subject who undecides himself, and for whom the decision of his discourse is continually undecided. There is no chance of escaping from the metaphysical-anthropological reconstruction of the Subject, without the irruption of this whisper. And no philosophical work is of any interest, unless it is carried out in order to run this risk—and not merely to discourse about it.

But this gesture itself—the only one by which something might reach us of what is coming about—passes through discourse (even though it does not *only* involve that). If Blanchot's name and his text would let some fear and others hope that we are trying to insinuate that philosophy is (simply) a kind of literary practice, that is, more generally, a kind of artistic practice (and here again in the simple, albeit modern, sense of the term), it is necessary, however paradoxical it might seem, to complete Blanchot's sentences with the following ones by Adorno:

> A philosophy that tried to imitate art, that would turn itself into a work of art, would be expunging itself. . . . Common to art and philosophy is not the form, not the forming process, but a mode of conduct that forbids pseudomorphosis. Both keep faith with their own substance through their opposites: art by making itself resistant to its meanings; philosophy, by refusing to clutch at any immediate thing. . . . [Philosophy] must strive, by way of the concept, to transcend the concept.[20]

This gesture therefore involves discourse, which is not to say only theorizing. It involves the imperative of having to confront the *dis-course* within discourse, which is the only chance of ever being faced with what withdraws behind the Subject, what or whom undecides itself as subject. It is therefore necessary again to pass through the discourse by means of which the Subject was decided: the metaphysical discourse, with which, especially in this capacity, we can never be in the clear. And in the context of the present book, this can only mean Descartes's discourse, this discourse—and this *Discourse*—to which, as we have pointed out, certain analytical remarks must be traced as if irresistibly—while the linguistic discourse of the subject of the utterance inevitably comes up against it and against its *cogito*.[21]

However, there will be no question of installing ourselves again in Descartes and in his foundation of the Subject, nor of manifesting a discursive power superior to his—or a power of the philosophical superior to that of the linguistic or psychoanalytical. (It is even in this difference with regard to theoretical power that the specificity of the philosophical gesture must first of all manifest itself.) There will also be no question of unveiling a truth of Descartes—be it that of an abyss or a fissure—that would hide behind all these discourses, as if it were their ground. It will rather be a matter of reaching the place, indeed of going back to the instant of a foundation, that of the Subject—in order to lend an ear to what only the foundation can make audible, because it triggers it and brings it about: the whisper of the subject that utters itself there, and collapses there. If philosophical discourse "is perhaps only an inexorable manner of losing and of losing oneself,"[22] as Blanchot again writes, this can only be verified, *as a matter of principle*, there where this discourse posits itself as its own self-utterance, or better as its self-performance, a (uttered or uttering) position that is explicit in Descartes, but one that carries out a program inscribed since Parmenides as *the* very program of our discourse, a program without which no anthropological subject, and no psychoanalytic upheaval of the "Me" would have been possible. But what happens to this program is also that it programs its own downfall—which is something different than exposing itself to critique, to theoretical overcoming, or to anthropological forgetting.

To one who utters—and denounces—itself in this way, we will let it be called and call itself *ego*. This will be a nomination, neither that of a *me*, nor that of an *I*.[23] It will not give rise to an egology, neither a transcendental nor an undecidable one. But, starting from the origin of egology and from the egological origin, it will attempt to hear what *calls itself* while uttering itself, not even an already formed path, but the uttering from which a whisper comes out or seeps out, always untimely and inactual—and which calls *us*.

Let us start all over again, then, as if we had not said anything yet.

II. . . . Vel mente concipitur

Descartes imprints the mark of certainty onto three centuries of modernity. We are still there. It is not a matter, as is well known, of the trivial certainty (pure conviction) of some kind of subjectivism, let alone of this absurd invention that is called the "Cartesian mind." It is a matter of this *terra firma*, this solid ground on which Hegel says thought lands with Descartes,[24] or of what Husserl calls "the Cartesian primal establishment [*Urstiftung*] of the entire philosophical modernity."[25] In other words, it is a matter of the foundation [*assise*] or the substrate of thought that is finally brought to light within thought itself and *as* thought. In yet other terms, it is a matter of the Subject—the *subjectum* as *quod substat*, and of truth as certainty insofar as truth is established within the position and according to the structure of the *substratum*, the latter henceforth understood as the substratum *of representation*, as that for which and through which something in general can be represented (thought)—and thereby as *the one* for whom and by whom something can be thought.

The Heideggerian commentary on Descartes is here easily recognizable. It is constantly presupposed in these pages, just as it is presupposed that the Heideggerian commentary does not constitute one "interpretation" of Descartes among others but the inevitable elucidation of his thought. These premises are not arbitrary: it will become clear that our analyses can only attempt to extend beyond the Heideggerian commentary insofar as they also confirm it. Confirmed by what follows, let us only state this: the Heideggerian analysis is exclusively one of the *cogito*, and it is exactly as such that it can only be confirmed. But as such it bypasses in a surprising way the precogitative and matricial statement, so to speak, which declares: *ego sum*. It is here that an interrogation of the subject-uttering-itself has to depart from an analytic of the subject-of-representation.[26] Heidegger brings himself to the edge of this gap when he comes to write: "Thus the *proposition* [*der* Satz] of the *cogito sum* is the subiectum—not the wording of the proposition, or the proposition considered as a grammatical construct, or taken in its supposedly neutral 'meaningful content' that can be thought in itself, but rather the 'proposition' considered according to what is expressed [*ausspricht*] as essentially unfolding there, and as what supports it in its proper essence as a proposition."[27] Nevertheless, Heidegger immediately determines this essence as the essence of representation. Hence, the gap that now appears to us to impose itself consists in interrogating not the essence, but the *proposing* or the *proposer* [le proposant], so to speak, of the proposition: *ego* uttering itself. Which amounts to the same thing as interrogating the "essence" (if there is still one) of the *first* proposition: "ego sum."

The certainty, thus understood as the propositional certainty of the *cogito*, articulates all of our discourses, even the most uncertain, including the vast majority of the modern discourses that have challenged "certainty," "representation," and the "subject." In all these discourses a "subject-of-representation" is at work: for example (this is perhaps also true of Heidegger's discourse), a subject-who-knows-what-is-happening-with-the-subject-of-representation, who knows how to represent it as the illusion of the presence-to-self of a consciousness, or as the subject of a phantasm, and who thus knows how to represent himself, that is, to present to himself the truth about Descartes as thinker of an illusory or phantasmatic subject-of-representation . . .

From all sides, then, whether as the subject-unconscious, or as subject-history, subject-language, subject-machine, subject-text, subject-body, or subject-desire (and everywhere where the subject is declared to be simple effect-of-subject), these new subjects have so far only produced the aggravation, or in a simpler and more massive way, the exacerbation of the *status* of the Subject: the consolidation of the *substratum* as such, which *substrates itself*, if one may say so, all the more and all the better now that it claims to sink deeper outside of the figure of the conscious subject, of the subject as creator or as master.

For this gesture of sinking amounts each time to pushing backward the general form of an *instance* that sustains and commands the possibility of assigning, from out of itself, all the figures of the subject, and to identify them (beginning with the weak, pallid, unsteady figure of the conscious subject, to which one likes to reduce the *cogito* so as to better laugh at or lament the extent of its unconscious, but also its obliviousness [*son inconscience*]). But it is clear that such an instance, whatever name it is given and wherever it is inscribed—on "another scene" or in a biochemical combinatorics— forms in such a way the proper *substance* of a new "cogito." It is to this instance that all the representations of "subjects" are related, and it is this instance that identifies them. (*Cogito*, after all, means *cum agito*, to put, squeeze or press together, together with oneself: but a *self* does not have to be a consciousness or a mind; it is a pole of identification.) Any operation of identification of a subject, even if it leads to an identity that is purely negative, critical, dissociative, or chaotic, is in the end itself *the* Subject, the true substratum.

This infinite regression was in fact already programmed by the *cogito*: As soon as truth as certainty entails the representative appropriation of the thing (or its presentation-to-self), one cannot stop sinking deeper toward an always prior appropriation of appropriation itself, toward a representation of representation, and toward a presentation-to-self of the truth of presentation-to-self. Spinoza understood this well and cut it short by declaring: "truth reveals its own self."[28] Perhaps no expression has remained more foreign to the modern world as this one, a world that has kept on digging, imperturbably, and in all seriousness, the infinite substratification of the Subject, without realizing that it was thereby carrying out the will of this Subject.

A strange forgetting, moreover, and a strange preservation . . . They say— or they do not say anymore, but in recent years thought has come to a standstill (at least the thought that makes the most noise) by heavily insisting upon this: "not *I* think, but *it* thinks." They say (it says?): "it works everywhere, sometimes continuously and sometimes on and off. It breathes, it heats up, it eats. It shits, it fucks." And they immediately add: "What a mistake to have ever said *the* id."[29] And it is undoubtedly a mistake to say *the* id. But it is perhaps also a mistake to *say* "*it*," and our vigilance still appears to be a little bit limited; for it is not the definite article that alone produces substantification. We know very well, at least since Nietzsche, that the substance relates to the subject of the verb (whatever the exact nature of this dependency or this adherence might be), and it is this substance that is already at work in the "it works everywhere." Why forget that Nietzsche, after having substituted "it thinks" for "I think," adds:

> In fact, there is already too much packed into the "it thinks": even the "it" contains an *interpretation* of the process, and does not belong to the process itself.[30]

Even if, in turn, we might have to go beyond Nietzsche's expression and interrogate the interpretation that is also contained in "the process itself" (thinks, works, breathes . . . as if that could work without subject . . .), and in its claim to constitute an ultimate authority, we still want to place everything that follows, at least provisionally, under the rubric of this Nietzschean demand, the only rigorous one—and the only one that might guide us toward what is missing, that is, toward an *untimely examination* of the subject.

Not without knowing that its untimeliness rushes us at once to the extreme edge of discourse, and that it exhausts the resources of discourse even before discourse has been allowed to begin, or in the very opening of its first incision. It is there that we must work, in this exhaustion, where the Subject perhaps exhausts itself.

But it will not be to seek refuge in the unsayable, or on the other side of discourse. We know—"we" here does not mean the author, but all of us, we all know, without always wanting to know it—we know all too well that a different and identical cohort of Subjects has already preceded us there: Figure or Gesture, Scream or Signifier, Psychosis or Poetry. We know it so well that we have very quickly worn out the novelty of these so-called *self-* saying nonsubjects—we have despaired of their theoretical and aesthetic, practical and political virtues—and that many now allow themselves to declare, with a certain relief: "no one can escape the Subject, he rules the world!" while others (or the same ones) are simply beginning to revive the most classical and most unsophisticated figure of the individual subject, inner consciousness of itself and of its freedom.

If it is on the contrary a matter of accompanying and interrogating the exhaustion of the Subject (or rather, undoubtedly, of letting ourselves be placed into question by this exhaustion, which has befallen us), we will inscribe Nietzsche's demand in order to ask this single question: What if Nietzsche, at this point, came closest to the foundation of the Subject, closest to Descartes? What if he came close to it not only in the manner established by Heidegger (that is, in (re)founding absolutely the metaphysics of subjectity as "metaphysics of the absolute subjectivity of the Will to Power"[31]), but also, and conversely, because Nietzsche's gesture, by the very fact that it accomplishes "the end of metaphysics," enables us to question what in Descartes's thought, in the thought of the Subject, *has already started to bring* the metaphysics of the Subject *to an end*.

In still other words, it is a matter of questioning what *in principle finishes* the Subject, of questioning a (de)constituting end, the finish or finitude of *ego*.

Heidegger defines the "end of metaphysics" as "the historical moment in which *the essential possibilities* of metaphysics are exhausted."[32] All I am proposing is to verify the following statement: *the Cartesian establishment of the Subject corresponds*, through the most binding necessity of its own structure, *to the instantaneous exhaustion of its essential possibilities.*

The *very* erection and inauguration of the Subject will have brought about the collapse of its substance. Not only have they brought it about but the collapse of the substance also *belongs* to the erection of the Subject. Or again: *ego sum* has never posited itself except by means of *cogito*, and *cogito* (what a mistake to have said *the* cogito . . .) has never taken place but by means of its extreme point, which is that of "a singular and unprecedented excess—an excess in the direction of the nondetermined, Nothingness or Infinity, an excess which overflows the totality of that which can be thought."[33] To which we will add: an excess that overflows, originarily and before *everything*, the very possibility of thinking thought itself. An excess that overflows, then, the very possibility of thought plain and simple, one might say, to the extent that the reflexive or speculative redoubling of thought implies nothing other, to begin with—and to begin *itself*—than the pure (but not simple) identity of thought. Such an identity would then exceed itself.

Here again it is perhaps through Spinoza that we would have to pass: the identity of thought is the identity of the "true idea," which reveals itself through itself. And if the *cogito* continues to harass the true idea—if something of Descartes, or some*one* of him, insists and resists within Spinoza—it is not because the *cogito* would impose an infinite self-reflection (which Descartes would, incidentally, also reject). It would be because the *cogito* brings about the collapsing and overflowing of thought in its very establishment, in its very identification, or because it brings about an overflowing of truth in its own "patefaction."

Thus, the problem is clear, even if it is not simple: Descartes refuses nothing more persistently than to introduce a thought of thought, a reflectivity within the cogito.[34] On the other hand, he neither authorizes us nor leads us to simply contemplate the revelation of the true.[35] And under the cover of a dubious use of the term "intuition," he does not allow either that we introduce in any way some kind of intimate, vaguely psychological or existential, assent to a *self* (the "self" of a "self-consciousness") in the "ego sum," since doubt suspends exactly such an assent.[36] For this triple reason, it is impossible at the utmost limit where Descartes holds himself, if he indeed holds himself there, to grasp thought, that is, the Subject, and yet it is here that thought sets itself up as Subject.

In other words, what is necessary starting from here is to try to reach, or at least to approach, the point of this setting up, insofar as certainty is both grasped and concealed at this point in the *same* gesture. But, by definition, this point can neither be reached nor approached. Perhaps it is not even a point—or perhaps there is in this point no point at all.

Or else, and in order to refer to that by which idealism will later seek to provide an answer to the problem, it is a matter of experiencing and putting to the test [*éprouver*] how the Cartesian Subject is posited *and* is not posited as *intellectual intuition*, and hence how it is *and* is not offered in the visual speculation of itself, in the *theory* of its being-Self: sight devoid of transparency, face deprived of eyes as well as of mirror.

One might reply that in appealing to the impossibility of intellectual intuition, we are presenting Descartes in the guise of Kant. But aside from the fact that Descartes, as we will see, is no stranger to masks, it is not exactly wrong to believe that we are here examining how Descartes rigorously controls the principle of Kantian critique, inasmuch as the stake of this critique remains, to this day, the irremediable crisis of the Subject (and it is a matter of something completely different than a Cartesian prehistory of Kantism as it prevails in certain traditions of interpretation). Such a "principle," however, will only be able to be grasped well if we first take the measure of all that separates Descartes from Kant, that is, of the gap between the setting up of the Subject and its crisis. The gap is to be measured on the basis of the following: With Kant, intuition and concept are separated from the start, and intuition is itself divided from itself; with Descartes, thought is set up as an identity prior to any distinction between intuition and concept; thought is installed, if one wants, as the intuition of its concept. Yet, it is *within* the genesis of this identity that this identity collapses. This is what happens to it, and what we must still recognize. The identity is hollowed by its own opening, which the *Critique* will have as its extraordinary task to *measure*, as one measures a space or gap. In order for this task to be undertaken—which we will have to discuss elsewhere—the Subject had to have opened itself up. In this empty opening—eye and mouth, as we will see, seeing mouth, speaking eye, muted eye, blind mouth—the Subject is *depos(it)ed*, in all senses of the word. The Subject lays down [*dépose*] its certainty on the edge of this open gap.

The four essays that follow are four attempts at treading this limit, this edgeless opening that delimits the Subject and where the Subject overflows itself—or within which its identity withdraws and distinguishes itself.

These four paths are discontinuous: the topic is not a general and systematic theory of Cartesianism. It goes over the same point again and again—the Cartesian point of the *Same*—in order to confirm that the Subject does not hold itself there, neither as the One, nor as the Other. But indeed as the Same, for the Same has as its innermost and most exorbitant nature to *undecide itself.* This is why *ego sum* exhausts, in being uttered and because it is uttered, in the instant of its uttering, any essence of subject.

What happens to the one who cannot sustain himself by means of an essence? In other words, *what is man?*—this is the question to which the last of our paths will lead us, Kant's fourth question, which Kant claims philosophy cannot answer (why then do those who make man speak so loudly in their "philosophy" today stubbornly ignore this question?). Descartes, in opening man up, has initiated the epoch of the impossible answer *about the subject* of man. And perhaps, as a result, an epoch could be initiated in which man is the one to whom something *happens*, something commensurate with what he is not, commensurate with this: that he is not. Something of the kind that befalls you (us) unexpectedly: an accident, a news, an order. A question of actuality, a question of the untimely actuality of "man."

What occurs to the subject, what befalls it—instead of supporting it with a sub-stance, and even instead of supporting it with a word—is, in the end, as we will see, its *areality*, according to the concept that I have started to develop elsewhere.[37] The term suggests both lack of reality (which is not an absence, and makes it impossible to carry out a negative egology in the fashion of negative theology) and area—*area* in Latin—the quality of space and extension prior to any spatiality. Areality is not the transcendental form of space either; prior to the transcendental regime (but only thinkable on the basis of Kant), more "primitive," areality extends itself as the unascribable place of the formless experience the "subject" has of its "own" chaos. Precisely because it has thought the absolute subjectity of substance, Descartes's thought keeps, at every instant, seeing—without seeing anything—this experience befalling it unexpectedly. The unexpectedness, the im-pro-vision (and perhaps also the improvisation that accompanies any appearing on the scene), the obscurity prior to any vision and the excess of clarity *itself* over clarity—all this is nothing other than the areality that occurs to the subject who says *ego sum*, saying in turns:

ego sum, *dum scribo*
ego sum—*larvatus pro Deo*—
ego sum: *mundus est fabula*,
ego sum *unum quid* . . .

Dum Scribo

... *dum scribo*—"while I am writing," writes Descartes in the twelfth of the *Rules for the Direction of the Mind*.[1]

While I am writing these Rules, which have as their sole object to secure for the human mind, once and for all, its unique and constant direction toward the truth, toward the genuine science, that is, toward this *Mathesis universalis*, the knowing of which is less a knowing of something (a content, a result, for example the number produced through a mathematical operation) than the knowing of the structure and the procedure of knowing itself, of its operativity, the knowing, as I will write in my sixteenth Rule, not of the "sum" but of the manner in which the sum "depends on the data" (458/61)—and for you who are reading me in order to take cognizance of this knowledge, it is less a matter of knowing what I write than the manner in which I write it. The Mathesis is the knowledge of the procedure, of the *quomodo, in quo tamn uno scientia proprie consistit*: It is in this procedure that science is posited and composed, is gathered and brought into its own.[2]

While I am writing this book, the first one that I am truly writing in the manner of a book, but which I will nevertheless never finish or publish: not because of an error of thinking that I am putting into it, but rather because "while I was working on [it] I acquired a little more knowledge than I had when I began [it], and when I tried to take account of this I was forced to start a new project, rather larger than the first. It is as if a man began building a house and then acquired unexpected riches and so changed his status that the building he had begun was now too small for him," as I write to Mersenne on April 15, 1630.[3] As I will show you, I will have to find accommodation in a more spacious, less confining book.

While I am writing in these notebooks, on these *codices* (*Codices novem de Regulis* . . . , says the Stockholm inventory, nine notebooks of useful and clear rules for the direction of the mind in the search for truth): The Ancients wrote on the scroll, the *volumen*, the Moderns on the notebook, that is, for some, the *codicarium*, the small *codex*, and for others, more learned, the *quaternum*, a codex made of four sheets. I am writing on the *codex*, the paper of which does not close up on itself in the process of involution as is the case with the volume, but offers the plane of its surface always ready in advance for writing as for reading. Its leaves are turned one after the other and can be numbered, making reading and writing easier in all respects, as befits the epoch that I am inaugurating and that will be the epoch of a "practical philosophy" intended to "make ourselves, as it were, the lords and masters of nature."[4] The *codex* is a piece of wood—from the stump or trunk—of that very wood from which the *liber*, between the bark and the sapwood, will make the book. The *codex* consists of sheets of wood joined at the back, and hence bound and articulated one upon the other. It is a writing machine suited for connecting all the monstrative and demonstrative principles of knowledge in the clearest, simplest, and most rigorous way. I am writing its rules, I am drawing up its code; I am making a book, I am codifying the Truth, I am making it inseparable, indissociable, and indiscernible from the operation that here and now inscribes its rules. I am making the first book of knowledge that knows itself in the act and manner of inscribing itself.

While I am writing without knowing that I will keep these nine notebooks and carry them with me to Stockholm, where they will be found among my papers after my death and sent to Clerselier in France—but before reaching him they will have sunk in the Seine with the boat that was transporting them from Rouen to Paris, they will have spent three days in a chest at the bottom of the river (in the same state as I was when I started the Second Meditation: "It feels as if I have fallen unexpectedly into a deep whirlpool which tumbles me around so that I can neither stand on the bottom nor swim up to the top"[5]), and on the third day "God permitted that they be found again,"[6] and they will have been fished out and dried, to be first recopied and sent to several learned persons, and then published in my *Opuscula posthuma* of 1701. And even though I do not know this story, it is nonetheless true that I write what I do not publish so that it can be read after my death (as it will be said in the *Discourse*).[7] My other motive for taking "as much care over these writings as I would if I intended to have them published" is that "undoubtedly we always look more carefully at something we think is to be seen by others."[8] While I am writing I believe to see myself being seen by many others, who are reading over my shoulder the words traced by the hand of a dead man immobilized for all eternity, the eternity of truth, in the instant of its inscription: *dum scribo . . .*

Dum scribo, intelligo . . . —while I am writing, I understand. Intellection is the collection, the gathering [*recueil*] of what must be selected, discerned: *inter-lectio*. It is *reading* [la lecture]: I read with intelligence while I am writing, I read between my lines. I am writing, but the intellect grasps well beyond writing what there is to be read, what makes of what is written a book, the Book of the Rules of the Mind, the Book of Intellection. I collect the spirit of the book, just as an attentive reader can do—*facile colliget attentus Lector* (416/49), one of those who will know how to consider and respect, as I have been demanding since my fourth Rule, the exact meaning which is mine here—*quicumque . . . attente respexerit ad meum sensum* (374/17)—the meaning of this Mathesis that is without common measure with any other kind of knowledge. It goes without saying that I understand between my own lines, it goes without saying that I should remain, in that instant and until my death immortalizes its inscription, my best, my most attentive, and my only reader.

It goes without saying, therefore, that what I understand so well cannot be anything but myself. This must not be taken as a metaphor, as if by it I meant "my doctrine" or "my thought" (nor do I mean what all my other readers will say, not having been able to read while I was writing, and hence not being perfectly attentive, when they will declare: This is Descartes, this is his method). You will see that here nothing must be taken figuratively, nothing must be understood by means of figures. I read between my lines: It is not what I write that I understand while I am writing, but I understand, or rather I gather that *I am writing.* I collect myself in writing. *Cogito, sum,* as it will be written later; here I am writing *scribo, intelligo.*

I collect myself writing my code, and it is in this instant that I am tracing the knowledge of it—while I am tracing the knowledge of this gesture. It is the moment to be attentive:

> *dum scribo, intelligo eodem instanti quo singuli characteres in charta exprimuntur, non tantum inferiorem calami partem moveri, sed nullum in hac vel minimum motum esse posse, quin simul etiam in toto calamo recipiatur* (414)

> While I am writing, I understand that at the very moment when individual letters are traced on the paper one after the other, it is not only the lower part of the pen that is moving, but that there cannot be even the slightest movement in that lower part that is not simultaneously taking place in the whole pen (41).

I collect my writing: the movement of my pen. This movement takes place on occasion of the tracing of the letters according to their outline. This tracing is successive and discrete: *singuli,* one by one the characters are inscribed. Even though I am writing by hand, with a joined-up script of the type that is normally called cursive, it is not the flow that interests me. It is the instant when a character singles itself out: My model is a typographical one, like that of a printer—I am a writing machine, a typewriter. *Characteres exprimuntur*: In every instant, in the unity of the instant, one character is expressed. I do not break down the letters in distinctive features of a lower order, and thereby I only measure the instant by means of the letter. The instant is not a chronological measure; it is quite evidently the achronic limit of such a measure. As such, it constitutes a characterological or graphological measure (the two sciences go together): This instant is the unit of presentation of a figure and of only one. Reciprocally, the figure—the distinct and distinctive outline in which the very individuality of something or someone is singled out, traced out, and presented—is what is given as unique and complete in the instant. The character is expressed in the figure, which amounts to saying that it is imprinted.

While I am writing, at each instant, the distinctive mark of a phonematic unit of the language is imprinted: The printed whole of this phonography will not constitute a duration, since it will be a sum of characterological units. The sum will be characteristic: It will constitute the impression of the figure of thought expressed by language, the impression of the true Rule of Truth, my Book.

This is imprinted in *charta*, on the charter—for centuries already this old word, this Greek word for paper, has been privileged to designate legal deeds, establishing rights, and sanctioning agreements. The *paper* par excellence is always the title, the attestation, the legal presence. Here is the charter of science: It has no other signature and seal than the character of its graphy.

(Charter or map [*carte*], it is the same thing: I will sign René Des Cartes.)

The movement of this writing draws the outline of the letters: The mind is nowhere but there. But it is not there because of the mediation of the signs that I trace out. It is there *as* the movement of my pen, and this movement is not considered here—by me, who produce and understand it—as the instrument of the deposition of a signification. What I collect while I am writing stops at the edge of the writing that makes sense; it only lightly touches the signs. Of writing, what must be considered here, with me, is only its nonsignifying gesture.

This gesture is instantaneously the same in the whole pen; in the instant, that is, without passage, transfer, progression, or communication: *recipiatur*, it is received, localized, imparted in one stroke from the bottom to the top of my pen. *Dum scribo*: not for the duration of my writing toil, but within the *same* time, and consequently outside of duration, outside of writing too: I am writing without writing in the instantaneity of the movement, describing each time various movements that are subjected to the same instantaneity.

atque illas omnes motuum diversitates etiam a superiori ejus parte in aëre designari,
etiamsi nihil reale ab uno extremo ad aliud transmigrare concipiam (414)

[and I understand and gather] that all these various movements are traced out
in the air by the tip of the pen, even though I do not conceive of anything real
passing from one end to the other (41).

The extremes meet in the instant. In the air, in a transparent writing,
impalpable and invisible, a true etherography, the snapshot—the photographic "instantaneity"—of my movement of writing is traced. The extremes touch, the impression happens by contact, and the Book of truth is
drawn in the purity of the air: *designari* designates not the sign but the de-
sign of the *signum*, mark, stamp, character, or seal. The Book is sealed with
an aerial wax, the Book is itself the seal of the instant affixed to the copresence of the parts of the pen with which I am writing what I understand—
and which is nothing other than the very sealing of the seal.

For what I expose in this twelfth rule is the truth of the seal. In it, I collect
and conclude all the preceding Rules. I put to work *in genere*—in a completely general and generic way—the principles of true knowledge, about
which I have established that it takes place above all through intuition,
the vision of the thing in the natural light of the mind, the luminous and
characteristic impression with which I am struck.

Come back to the beginning of the Rule. There I recall that only the
intellect—*solus intellectus*—is capable of perceiving the truth—*percipiendae
veritatis est capax*: is capable of the truth that has to be perceived, as it must
be translated word for word. It is a matter of the *capacitas* of the intellect, of
its quality as receptacle, of what it can receive and contain. It is a matter of
the intellect as *collection* [recueil], collection of imprinted marks as I will
show—and hence of the intellect in its supreme quality as Book.

I have written in my third Rule that by *intuition* "I do not mean the fluc-
tuating testimony of the senses or the deceptive judgement of the imagination as it botches things together" (368/14). Intuition is a pure vision, a pure
vision of the mind. Without removing any of its purity, here I want *to make*

it see and be seen [la faire voir]: understand this in all its senses. This is why I write:

> *Solus intellectus equidem percipiendae veritatis est capax, qui tamen juvandus est ab imaginatione, sensu, et memoria, ne quid forte, quod in nostra industria positum sit, omittamus* (411)

> . . . but the intellect has to be assisted by imagination, sense-perception and memory if we are not to omit anything which lies within our industry (39).

The intellect does not function without this whole machine. Industry is what we dispose, arrange, prepare, or manufacture in ourselves (*endo-struo*). The industrial revolution is the revolution of the subject. The subject is not a pure mind: It is the pure mind that puts to work, within itself, the machine— the machine for imprinting images. It is the engineer *ad directionem ingenii.*

My intellection requires the industry of images: My reading is the collection of charts, schemas, tables, figures, and maps that I can read between the lines. Designs, over and above signs, are the closest and most suitable aids of the mind. They are part of its factory; this factory is that of a body; this industrious body receives images—and not signs; it receives *signa*, signatures or seals. No thought is more material than mine: My Knowledge needs the whole physical machine whose forces imprint forms. The image is for me less a copy, a simulacrum, or an icon of some transcendent reality than the truth as the instantaneous *impression* of certainty upon my mind. Certainty is the collection of what is separated, distinguished, defined, discerned. It matters little that "*imagine*" has the same root as "*imitate*"; admittedly, I will never say that to imagine is to conceive, but nevertheless, I want to grasp "to imagine" via the root of "to imprint"—to press, apply, and imbed in myself the certain figure of any conceivable thing. My knowledge will be bookish or will not be. And this is what I want to make see and be seen.

To this end,

> *optarem exponere hoc in loco, quid sit mens hominis, quid corpus, quo modo hoc ab illa informetur* (411)

> I should like to explain at this point what the human mind is, what the body is and how it is informed by the mind (39–40).

I should like to explain how the mind gives the body its figure, how the body is the figure that the mind traces for itself, and thus leads you by a demonstrative path to grasp in a clear light the true mode of knowledge. I wish that—

Cupio enim semper ita scriber (411)

Indeed, I always desire to write in such a way as to put forward *easdem rationes, quae me eo deduxerunt* (412): the reasons that have led me there, the reasons that have *deduced* me to the truth. I desire that my writing be my deduction, and yours (which could also be your seduction: *et quibus existimo alios etiam posse persuaderi* [412]). I desire my writing constantly as the true persuasion of deduction by reasons. It is in this way that I would like to expose *hoc in loco* the information of my body: I thereby desire the seduction of my writing body, or, but it would amount to the same thing, I desire the deduction of the writer that I am—

nisi nimis angustus mihi videretur (411): were it not for the fact that this locus seems to me to be too confining. I lack the necessary space for my deduction. Here: in my book. My book is too confined. My notebooks, my codices, my maps are too tight. The places of writing form narrow passes, passages that are impassable for the exposition of the writing body of the mind. *Locus nimis augustus: angor*, I am strangled there, my desire gets anxious there, my pen is squeezed in the corner of a writing unequal to the truth.

The book is not too confining because it is too small: "even if all the knowledge that can be desired were contained in books, the good things in them would be mingled with so many useless things, and scattered haphazardly through such a pile of massive tomes, that we should need more time for reading them than our present life allows, and more intelligence for picking out the useful material than would be required for discovering it on our own."[9] This is what I will later put at the head of a little dialogue that I will call *The Search for Truth by Means of the Natural Light*, which I will not complete and which will appear, likewise, among the *Opuscula posthuma*.

The book is too confining because it must be read: What I would like to show you is not to be read but seen. I desire an illuminating, blinding writing. I want to write with light, and what I am desperately trying to communicate to you is my photograph, taken while I am writing.

So I will not explain how the body is informed by the mind. Rather I will explain how the mind makes itself seen in the body, or how one and the other take shape together—in the writing that imprints itself. But it is perhaps in this way, by explaining to you its impression, that I will escape the restricted volume of this book.

For it is still necessary to conquer the Writing of the Book, to get out of the corner and the anguish. If you don't mind, we will at the very least exert the best of our industry on it.

You do not have to believe, if you do not wish to believe it, that things are in reality as I will describe them: *sed quid impediet quominus easdem suppositiones sequamini*—"But what is to prevent you from following these suppositions" if they make *omnia longe clariora* (412), "everything much clearer?" (40). Hence we will make suppositions, and we will judge the strength of the supports by the sight of the façade, once it is erected. The sup-position will take on a sub-stantial value from the moment it lets us see. The visible will decide for the invisible, and the impression of the letter for the exposition of the mind.

Concipiendum est igitur: Here then is what must be conceived:

sensus omnes externos . . . proprie . . . sentire per passionem tantum, eadem ratione qua cera recipit figuram a sigillo (412)

all our external senses . . . strictly speaking . . . sense only by way of a passion, in the same way in which wax takes on an impression from a seal (40).

Sigillum, little *signum*, figurine or statuette, image borne by a seal. The world is not a world of signs but one of *signa* and *sigilla*. Seals imprint figures in the wax of the senses. The one who acquires knowledge of the world is the one who is sigillated. The treatise of Science—the one I am writing— is a general Sigillography, treatise of the seals of the World and of the wax of Man. I will keep this seal in mind, and I will imprint it in the Meditation of my thinking existence. In this Meditation, I will establish that the wax itself is known solely through my mind. You, who are reading my text after my death, in a single glance, you already know this famous passage:

Sed ecce, dum loquor, igni admovetur: saporis reliquiae purgantur, odor expirat, color mutatur, figura tollitur . . .

But while I am speaking, I put the wax by the fire, and look: the residual taste is eliminated, the smell goes away, the colour changes, the shape is lost . . . [10]

Dum loquor, while I am speaking, the wax melts, the shape is effaced, there remains only the conception I have of the wax, and "it is not the faculty of imagination that gives me my grasp of the wax."[11] I do not contradict this, even though I muster all the help of the imagination. But it is necessary to understand with what purity I already conceive the wax and the imagination here.

For here, *dum scribo,* while I am writing, the same wax is now on the brink of cooling and hardening itself; it is moved away from the fire, the seal is brought close. The wax receives the imprint of the figure, the passion of the senses renders me cognizant. In the later text, I will say what of the figure must be conceived. Here I am writing what must be figured of the conception; in the one as in the other case, it is a matter of imprinting the truth.

Neque hoc per analogiam dici putandum est; sed plane eodem modo concipiendum (412)

It should not be thought that I have a mere analogy in mind here: we must think [of it] in exactly the same way (40).

Do not imagine that I am speaking figuratively. There is nothing to imagine here but imagination itself; and thus the imagination would not, as it does elsewhere, engage in "false compositions."[12] And the imprint of the figure is neither an image nor a figure: It is properly the mode of the passion of the senses, and more particularly, as I specify at once, of the passion of the eye (*ita recipere figuram impressam ab illumination* (412): The eye photographs the figures of the world).

It is therefore in the most proper sense that I say that all of our external knowledge must be conceived in this way, *cum nihil facilius sub sensum cadat quam figura: tangitur enim et videtur* (413)—"since nothing is more readily

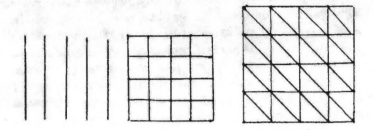

Rule Twelve (AT X 413)

perceivable by the senses than shape, for it can be touched as well as seen" (40). Understand that this happens here entirely literally: The figure is visible *for itself* [se *voit*]; it is the speculation of the figure. And for the figure, to see itself is to touch itself; it speculates itself without a mirror, making an impression on itself. The figure folds upon itself in imprinting itself here, in the passion of my eye, the figure of my vision. My eye touches itself, conceives itself.

I am not reading—I am writing and seeing. I see that everything takes shape—*quod tam communis et simplex sit figurae conceptus, ut involvatur in omni sensibili,* "the concept of shape [figure] is so common and simple that it is involved in everything perceivable by the senses" (413/40). It suffices to develop it in order to have, each time, the photograph of the figure of the thing. I can make you see or conceive white, blue, red, as shown in the accompanying figure.

This tricolored emblem suffices to show you that all sensible differences are expressible, imprintable by means of the infinite multitude of figures. The figure is infinite, the figure is everywhere present—it imprints each thing in me. The figure is the element of all things: You cannot think anything about the world without thinking it. *Cogito, figuratur.*

For the imprint is instantaneously transported to another part of the body quae *vocatur sensus communis,* which we call the common sense. The figure which is common to everything passes into the sense which is common to all the senses—*eodem instanti et absque ullius entis reali transit* (414), in the same instant and "without any entity really passing from the one to the other" (41).

How is this done?

It is, as you will have understood, what I understand while I am writing, and what I grasp through the fact that I am writing:

plane eodem modo, quo nunc, dum scribo, intelligo

While I am writing the twelfth of these Rules, which have no other object than to assure the mind of its unique direction toward the truth, I am identifying within my writing gesture the mode of instantaneous transmission, without transit, which grants me in truth knowledge of the world.

Hence, in speaking of my pen, I have also not spoken by analogy. I collect the snapshot of my writing, of the outline of my figures—for example, my tricolored pictography. I grasp the movement of my whole pen as the modality of the passage of any figure in me. The etherography is the same thing as the knowledge of things by the common sense. The external senses stand in the same relation with the common sense as do the two extremities of my pen. To know, to write, it is the same thing, the same imprint, provided that one knows how to read between the lines, right at the calamus, and that one knows how to see what it designates: the drawing of its signature. I have showed it to you: The aerial wax of the Book is the same wax of which the common sense is made, and it behaves like sealing wax: *plane eodem modo.*

Quis enim putet minorem esse connexionem inter partes corporis humani, quam inter illas calami . . . (414)

Who then would think that the connection between the parts of the human body is less close than that between the parts of the pen? (41)

The human body, in its exteriors and its interior, in its multiplicity and its unity, holds itself like a pen, and no doubt more than a pen—formidable calamus[13]—

et quid simplicius excogitari potest ad hoc exprimendum? (414)

What simpler way of portraying the matter can be thought out? (41)

I do not speak figuratively, but by excogitation, by invention, imagination, fantasy, by thought-outside-of-itself. The Duc de Luynes will translate this word in my *Meditations* as "extravagance."[14] I extravagate outside of thought in order to think the impression of the figure in my thought, and it is in this way that I conceive properly the industry of thought. Not only do I collect the gesture of my writing, not only do I see myself writing, not only do I take the figure of a writer, but I fantasize my whole body as a pen: my body—manipulated by myself, between my fingers, dactylographied body— moves with the same movement as the characters. It is the truth of this writing that I am writing here, and that is traced out in the air of my intellection at the same time as on the charter of my science. It is here that the Book of Rules is written; the most striking impression of truth is expressed in it, the most simple expression, the most excogitated one is imprinted in it. The true idea finds its imprimatur in it—

For we must at any rate conceive that

> *sensum communem fungi etiam vice sigilli ad easdem figuras vel ideas, a sensibus externis puras et sine corpore venientes, in phantasia vel imaginatione veluti in cera formandas; atque hanc phantasiam esse veram partem corporis* (414)

> the "common" sense functions like a seal, fashioning in the phantasy or imagination, as if in wax, the same figures or ideas which come, pure and without body, from the external senses. The phantasy is a genuine part of the body (41–42).

Passion becomes imprinting, the same sensing body is also the writing body, the same wax takes on the metallic hardness of a seal. How is that possible? How is this transubstantiation carried out? How do the hollows and reliefs invert their disposition at the very same instant?

> *neque enim totus calamus movetur, ut pars ejus inferior; quinimo, secundum majorem sui partem, plane diverso et contrario motu videtur incedere* (415)

> Again, the pen as a whole does not move in exactly the same way as its lower end; on the contrary, the upper part of the pen seems to have a quite different and opposite movement (42).

It is thus still the pen that allows you to conceive how the body is sealed in itself to the mind, how bodies are imprinted in thoughts: *plane eodem modo, plane diverso et contrario motu*—what you must conceive is the motor contrariety within modal identity. *Concipiendum est*: It is what is having to be conceived.

This is likewise the place—place without narrowness, without corner, and without anguish, widely offered to the infinity of figures that it imprints for itself—the place of the transfiguration of bodies: There, figures instantly become ideas, they are pure and without bodies. Having come from the sensuous outside without passage or transfer of matter, having come without coming or changing location, they are instantaneously transmitted such as they are, incorporeal.

I had established in my ninth Rule the instantaneous transmission of motive power:

> *si quantumvis longissimi baculi unam extremitatem moveam, facile concipio*
> *potentiam, per quam illa pars baculi movetur, uno et eodem instanti alias etiam*
> *omnes ejus partes necessario movere, quia tunc communicatur nuda, neque in aliquo*
> *corpore existit, ut in lapide, a quo deferatur* (402)

> if I move one end of a stick, however long it may be, I can easily conceive that
> the power which moves that part of the stick necessarily moves every other
> part of it instantaneously, because it is the bare power which is transmitted at
> that moment, and not the power as it exists in some body, such as a stone which
> carries it along (34).

This very long stick was a prefiguration of my pen: You can imagine it as big as you wish; you can imagine that it is infinite. You can write with a stake: What happens on the paper is of no consequence so long as this makes you understand that the figures behave in the same way as power. They communicate and are communicated naked. Nudity must be conceived as the stripping away of the body: its disappearance; and the figure must be conceived as power, the tracing more than the traced outline. At the top of the pen, the bodily figure inscribes its nudity in the clouds [*nuées*].

And in my text, in the same manner, the figures of things have instantly become ideas. I have substituted one word for the other without passage or transfer between the two concepts. This is how my science is expressed, by displacements without transfers. I am writing with a long stick, and my style is that of the instantaneous metaphor. I have spirited away the material cloak of figures without having to demonstrate anything about this operation, just as I have understood in one stroke that the characters traced in ink become at once, at the other extremity of my pen, pure aerial writings. The ideal seal of figures does not for all that strike the corporeal extension of my fantastic or fanciful wax with any less vigor or precision.

It is in this way that I can think: *solus intellectus* is here imprinted in a body transfigured by its nudity, by the power of its nudity. Intellection needs this imagining industry, this pornography, because it is itself the naked figure, the truth, transfigured in its idea. Such will then be my meditation, that "when I distinguish the wax from its outward forms—take the clothes off, as it were, and consider it naked—then although my judgment may still contain errors, at least my perception now requires a human mind."[15]

And if it seems to you that I spoke only about my knowledge of sensible things, must I then remind you that I do so in order to gather all this industry of the senses and of the imagination in the service of the purest and most genuine intellection.

Immediately after this in this same Rule, I will speak to you about that force by which we properly know all things, and I will say that it is pure *spiritualis*—that it is purely spiritual, that is, it is not even like these ideas of sensible things, which are only pure because their body has been spirited away. Here then is what I will say about that form without any figure:

I will say that it is a *toto corpore non minus distinctam, quam sit sanguis ab osse, vel manus ab oculo* (415), "no less distinct from the whole body than blood is distinct from bone, or the hand from the eye" (42).

So I distinguish the mind from the body by means of the distinction between the parts of that body within which, however, everything is connected at least as intimately as the parts of the pen or the stick. After I have led you to conceive contiguity and copresence as far as the idea itself, I now ask you, *plane diverso et contrario motu*, to conceive the total distinction they contain. I measure the distance from the mind to the body by means of the fluid that runs all through the body, like the ink in the calamus—or else, in opposition to the eye that sees the figures, I designate this distance by the hand that touches and grasps . . . the pen or the figures. You must conceive this spiritual writing with blood, this hematography.

I will also say of this force, *unicamque esse*—that it is one in all its operations. It is the same mind that senses and understands, that receives and forms figures, that denudes the virgin wax and imprints its mark on it, that sees the world and writes the science of it.

> *In quibus omnibus haec vis cognoscens interdum patitur, interdum agit, et modo sigillum, modo ceram imitatur* (415)

> In all these functions the cognitive power is sometimes passive, sometimes active; sometimes imitating the seal, sometimes the wax (42).

The mind imitates. I am thus speaking figuratively here, or at least I am saying that the mind properly does what it does only by imitation, and hence by image—*Quod tamen per analogiam tantum hic est sumendum, neque enim in rebus corporeis aliquid omnino huic simile invenitur* (415): "But this should be understood merely as an analogy, for nothing quite like this power is to be found in corporeal things" (42).

There is no perfect similitude. There is not really any spiritual seal or wax. Hence, the mind must be conceived outside of the analogy of the seal; we must no longer imprint on it the seal of analogy:

> *si denique sola agat, dicitur intelligere: quod ultimum quomodo fiat, fusius exponam suo loco* (416)

> when it acts on its own, it is said to understand. How understanding comes about I shall explain at greater length in the appropriate place (42).

I will say how, in another place. It is elsewhere that I will unseal the analogy: in a place that will not be found in this book, in this little book—*hoc labellum*, says the fourth Rule—in a place that will not narrow the angle of any writing. I will say it in its place: in the aerial place where no letter is traced, by means of a movement reverse to that of the characters on the narrow paper.

I will *explain* it, I will *expose* it—you will see nothing there anymore, no figure, you will not lift any imprint there, but you will understand, reading the pure etherography with the book and your eyelids closed, you will understand what the sigillography has shown you here. In this place no more than in this other one, are you asked to decipher signs: All that must be conceived about conception has been stamped on you by an analogy. Conception must be conceived according to the impression in the virgin and naked wax.

As for the conception of nudity itself, the naked power of conception, it requires even in its proper place the insistent figure of the impression. For this place is here, in no other future than that of the instant: The place is at the top of the calamus. There you see the evanescent figure of an imprint without contours for an idea without character, in a wax that never hardens to take the shape of the monogram of any seal. There you will decipher the inverted writing, the antigraphy of a stick in the air.

The antigraphical characters are unknown to us: but it is precisely in this case that we must show some ingenuity and that we must excogitate. I have written it in my tenth Rule:

> *methodus . . . non alia esse solet, quam ordinis, vel in ipsa re existentis, vel subtiliter excogitati, constans observatio: ut si velimus legere scripturam ignotis characteribus velatam, nullus quidem ordo hic apparet, sed tamen aliquem fingimus* (404)

> the method usually consists simply in constantly following an order, whether it is actually present in the matter in question or is ingeniously excogitated. For example, say we want to read something written in an unfamiliar cypher which lacks any apparent order: what we shall do is to invent an order (35).

We forge, we feign, we fiction: *fingimus*, we figure and we figure ourselves out in this way. The method consists in imposing order and the figure of writing onto the antigraphical order of truth.

To conceive well, we must be helped by the supplement of a figure—the antigraphy is still a writing, and the naked truth is always already sealed.

> *His autem omnibus ita conceptis, facile colliget attentus Lector, quænam petenda sint ab unaquaque facultate auxilia, et quousque hominum industria ad supplendos ingenii defectus possit extendi* (416)

> If all these matters are conceived along such lines, the attentive reader will have no difficulty in gathering what aids we should seek to obtain from each of

these faculties and the lengths to which human endeavour can be stretched in supplementing the shortcomings of our native intelligence (43).

Attentive readers of my Book, you have already conceived all this industry, provided that your concern for truth has led you, while reading me, to write yourselves. While you are writing, now, you understand, you collect thanks to the industry of your fantasy the penlike movement of your bodies. You see this calamus that you are, each part touching all the others, tracing in the upper air the characters—your characters—of the book that you are writing, where you collect the truth of what you are, the truth that you are—yet that you are while you are writing and only as long as you are writing. You see yourselves, you touch yourselves, you are figures, you figure yourselves. Thus you will have conceived with care *meum sensum*, the meaning of my book, the sense of common sense such as I imprint it: *scribo*, I write, I am writing, penman and wax figure.

My fundamental property lies in the immobility of my movement, in the death that in each instant interrupts and collects my writing gesture. It is the property of the pen, where nothing moves while the tracing takes place within its entire body. The structure of the calamus, whether it is quill or reed, must be that of a hollow body, so that it can hold the ink and let it flow. I am this hollow structure: Within me is the stripping of bodies, the blood that is spirited away, across my length is the sudden connection of a graphism. Such is my primary quality, the one that I have to conceive and that allows me to conceive, *plane eodem modo, plane diverso et contrario motu*. The imprint of its concept must be stamped: *calamitas*, nature of calamus, of cut straw: I am the chaff without wheat, without nourishing substance, as when a scourge strikes upon the harvest. I am a calamity.

This pen is unimaginable. But you have to conceive exactly what this means. It does not mean that we must imagine the unimaginable, that we must by force impose a figure on what does not have any. It does not mean, because of the faults and limits of our mind, that the figurelessness of pure intuition can only be given through a substitute of figure, and of writing. Rather, it means—according to what was already written by Montaigne, in whose book I read between the lines about divine beatitude—that we must *imagine* that the pure grasp of truth in its proper figure is *unimaginable*.[16]

The law of the proper figure is to figure from itself and in itself its own external limit, the unfigurable ring of its truth.

The truth of the soul is that of the pen. My *Principles* will establish it:

It can also be proved that the nature of our mind is such that the mere occurrence of certain motions in the body can stimulate it to have all manner of thoughts which have no likeness to the movements in question. This is especially true of the confused thoughts we call sensations or feelings. For we see that spoken or written words excite all sorts of thoughts and emotions in our minds. With the same paper, pen and ink, if the tip of the pen is pushed across the paper in a certain way it will form letters which excite in the mind of the reader thoughts of battles, storms and violence, and emotions of indignation and sorrow; but if the movements of the pen are just slightly different they will produce quite different thoughts of tranquillity, peace and pleasure, and quite opposite emotions of love and joy.[17]

Truth is a calamity.

Larvatus pro Deo

Bene latuit

Some reputations shine with such brilliance that they blind for a long time those who contemplate them—or believe themselves to do so.[1] Nothing is more famous, undoubtedly, within what might be called the ornamental history of modern philosophy than Descartes's saying, *"I come forward masked."* But nothing is more constant than the effects produced by this illustrious mask. Dazzled by such a declaration, commentators rush forward confidently. Some do so in order to remove the mask, without realizing that they do not know where to grasp it; others in order to locate it, thereby finding themselves forced to contrive this or that "secret Descartes," or more precisely to *feign* the *real* Descartes, that is, to put into play (as you will soon see) the most established and the most avowed of Descartes's procedures in regard to his "truth." Hence, they are trapped again by his mask.[2]

39

In fact, no one can claim to go further in this genre or to be better at it, and I do not propose to overcome such a necessary blindness. At the very most, we can propose to accept for a moment the singular face-to-face between a reader who does not see anything and the empty gaze of a mask. Let us read for the first time the famous text:

> Actors, taught not to let any embarrassment show on their faces, put on a mask. I will do the same. So far, I have been a spectator in this theatre which is the world, but I am now about to mount the stage, and I come forward masked [*larvatus prodeo*].[3]

A few lines later, as we know, Descartes writes: "*The mathematical treasure trove of Polybius, citizen of the world*" (AT X 213/I.2). This is the mask, then, the pseudonym intended for this first treatise that never saw the light of day. For us who know, the trick is exposed. Or so it is for the text of the 1620s: Under the name of Polybius, its author is Descartes. But just who is Descartes? And what if, after that, Descartes had never ceased to come forward masked? He had taken as his motto Ovid's saying: "*Bene vixit, bene qui latuit.*"[4] We must take the mask at its word, according to its maxim. In the end, we will have to read the pseudonymous text of the "Preliminaries" again.

To do so, a detour is necessary. We must first read through an anonymous text of 1637 titled *Discourse on the Method*.

Ut pictura

Descartes "formed a method," then, for "the search for truth," and he "venture[s] the opinion" that it is the only human occupation that "has solid worth and importance" (AT VI 3/I.12). Yet, such a declaration is not self-evident. On the contrary, what is self-evident, according to the very principles of Cartesian reform, is that this method cannot be cloaked in an argument based on authority. It can be presented only according to what should be called an argument based on *authorship*: That of which *I* alone am the author can impose itself only upon the judgment that each *I* will be able to pass upon it. This formula sums up the Cartesian mode and model of the communication of truth—a communication that is essentially dependent upon the very process whereby this truth is constituted as *certainty* (unless, in a more complex manner, this constitution depends in turn upon the very project of communicating truth. In a certain way, we must also concern ourselves with this here, that is, with the Cartesian inauguration of the modern obsession with communication, with the communication of truth and with communication *as* truth).

Accordingly, the truth/certainty of the method imposes a certain order upon its presentation. Eluding both the order of authority as well as the order of demonstration, what will have to be produced is the monstration of the author, or more precisely, of the "becoming-himself-author" (of the method).[5] This is why Descartes, having hardly announced his invention of method, immediately adds the following, which must provide the ordering scheme of the *Discourse*:

> Yet I may be wrong: perhaps what I take for gold and diamonds is nothing but a bit of copper and glass. . . . I shall be glad, nevertheless, to reveal in this discourse what paths I have followed, and to represent my life in it as if in a picture, so that everyone may judge it for himself; and thus, learning from public response the opinions held of it, I shall add a new means of self-instruction to those I am accustomed to using. (AT VI 3–4/I.112)

Taking glass to be diamonds is the act of a blind man. Descartes wrote it to Beeckman: "Imagine before your eyes a blind man so crazed by avarice that he spent entire days looking for precious stones among the refuse of his neighbour's house, and who, each time his hand came upon a small stone, or a small piece of glass, no sooner believed to have found a very precious stone."[6] We have here all of Descartes's fears—the fears of impropriety (a *false* treasure, drawn from *another*'s *refuse*)—and brought together under the supreme fear: that of blindness. The inability to see thrusts us into filth and alienation. If Descartes errs, then, it cannot be only a question of a partial error. It is all or nothing: clear-sightedness or blindness.

We shall not pause to consider the obviously rhetorical character of this "yet." It is clear that this qualm is *feigned*. But it is precisely the status and function of the feint that must be examined—a philosophical status and function that overdetermine rhetoric here, indeed that might even reverse or pervert it to the point of turning it into a *feigned rhetoric* . . . Let us then assume that Descartes must assure himself of the fact that he is not blind, that he sees what he touches, and that what he touches is not refuse but in truth gold.

To this end, he exhibits his own picture. "Representation" here does not denote a secondary, imitated copy, one that is consequently always more or less factitious, but rather presentation itself, the presentation of the thing itself. Descartes will expose himself, and the comparison with a picture allows him to summon up all the values of exactitude, authenticity, and of living presence that one can expect from a faithful portrait. Descartes presents his portrait, and the portrait is faithfulness itself, that is, what gives seeing itself. What is at stake in the *Discourse* is to make Descartes see and be seen [*faire voir*], to *give visibility and sight to the author of the method*. It turns out that this must be heard in all senses of the expression. We need not force the argument to show this.

It is indeed sufficient—and inevitable—to refer back to Descartes's avowed intentions regarding the exhibition of his picture. He wrote about them to Mersenne, in a letter informing him of the first draft of the *Meteorology*: "Moreover, please do not speak to anyone about this, for I have decided to publish this treatise as a specimen of my philosophy and to hide behind the picture in order to hear what people will say about it."[7]

The picture, the faithful picture, and if I may say so, the very faithfulness of the picture are in reality assigned with the mission of dissimulating from the public the author of the picture (and by the same token, its original). The Philosophy in question is not established by exposing itself—rather, it is exposed only to allow the author, while remaining hidden, to hear what one says about it.

The *Discourse* assigns to the picture the same function: to inform Descartes of the judgment of others, and hence to instruct him in his place of hiding. Since the *Discourse* is anonymous, the reader of 1637 knows that the author stands behind the painting. The dissimulation is not dissimulated; the feint is avowed. It remains a feint, however (with Descartes's feints, there are always one more and one less feint)—for what the letter says (but not the *Discourse*) is that Descartes does not believe in the frankness of others, and hence, from out of his hiding place, he hopes to take this frankness by surprise.[8]

The dissimulation of the author, the feint of his absence, provides him with the means of knowing by surprise which one he is: blind or clear-sighted. Could it be that Descartes counts upon this verification through the judgment of others? But how is it possible to veri-fy by this means what is established only in and through the author's exclusive certainty? The *Discourse* repeatedly denies its author access to a "new means of instruction" that comes from the outside. What comes to me from others belongs, as a matter of principle, to the same gnoseological level as everything the method is set up against: examples, customs, stories, fables. Thus, in Part Six, in superb contradiction with his prefatory declaration, Descartes will write: "But it has rarely happened that an objection has been raised which I had not wholly foreseen. . . . Thus I have almost never encountered a critic of my views who did not seem to be either less rigorous or less impartial than myself" (AT VI 68–69/I.146). From behind his picture, Descartes cannot expect anything, cannot hear anything that might amend his certainty.

And yet, this exposition might still be instructive. Indeed, it is perhaps only by means of such a device that Descartes can assure himself of his certainty, and hence, first of all, of the *cogito*. Perhaps the *cogito* can only *hear itself and be heard* by listening to those who behold its picture. If the truth of the portrait indeed resides in its conformity with the original, the dissimulation of this original implies that it is not *this* conformity that the viewers are expected to judge. Confronted with an unassignable and unverifiable resemblance, the viewers should pass judgment upon a conformity that is entirely contained within the picture, or that is created by it. They would have to repeat the famous *ut pictura poesis*, understanding it in the following way: The creation, the *poiesis* of truth takes the form of the painting through the subject of its authenticity. Nothing is less realist or naturalist than the pictorial aesthetic that can be derived from the *Discourse*, but nothing is less "aesthetic" than this painting, the representative function of which is from the outset indistinguishable from the presentation of its author. The author of the method can only present himself in painting— and this painting is at the same time its own original and the mask of the original who conceals himself, two feet away, behind his portrait. Standing before the picture, then, and commenting on it, the viewer would perhaps verify not the resemblance (insofar as the picture is a copy, its faithfulness is guaranteed *in principle* on account of the frankness and veracity of its author), but the very existence, the *sum* of the original. I am this thinking being that the other sees, or thinks she sees.

The resulting situation is a familiar one: In the Cartesian doctrine, it is homologous to the recognition of the existence of God by means of the vision of his idea (faithful copy) within me. The viewer of the picture sees Descartes as Descartes sees God (just as well, and hence, just as poorly). Such would be the use of this portrait positioned as a mask: *larvatus pro Deo*—I am masked in order to occupy God's place.

Videre videor

We are starting to suspect that this complex and artful device is not merely set up for our enjoyment. Or it is set up, precisely, for the sole purpose of guaranteeing a voyeuristic, that is, a *theoretical jouissance*. Here, the voyeur *listens* to some people—a kind of refinement of voyeurism—who are the viewers of his picture. The voyeur is thus also an exhibitionist. On account of this whole perverse montage, he obtains the desired vision of himself: theory. Neither rhetoric nor painting serves here to embellish or please: They obey the strictest necessity of a perversion that is put into play by the subject of the theory of the subject. This perversion is not accidental, but (as we will have to confirm) stems rather from this subject's constitution. Like other subjects, the subject of the theory of the subject is perverse by birth. Better: His birth is his perversion. I mask myself only in order to appear to myself and see myself, and to see myself hear.

This requires that we take into account all the operations and all the positions that are imposed by this perverse trajectory of the gaze.

Who *is watching* here, exactly? The viewer, of course, and the picture. The sightless eyes of the portrait watch whoever is looking at them. Descartes, for his part, does not see anything—except the obscure reverse of the canvas. But it is precisely in order to see, to see himself and hence to see whether he is blind or clear-sighted, that he must remain hidden from others and from his own portrait.

The optical model is not self-evident. It does not function within its own self-transparency, as we are accustomed to think (and not without reason) in relation to the Cartesian doctrine. Admittedly, optics possesses the privilege of all privileges for this *theory*. The *Optics*, which is introduced by the *Discourse*, begins with the following statement: "The conduct of our life depends entirely on our senses, and since sight is the noblest and most comprehensive of the senses."[9] Yet, within the *Optics* itself, access to vision—and to light—is only possible by means of a detour, and a detour through blindness. The famous comparison of the transmission of light with the movement of a stick not only includes a mechanical analogy; it also refers at the same time to the blind people's stick, about whom Descartes writes: "one might almost say that they see with their hands" (AT VI 84/I.153).[10] Contrary to what an entire tradition consecrated by August Comte has led us to believe, Descartes never lays claim to a self-vision—to a speculation—of the eye. Eye, light, and vision can only be seen through a blindness that constitutes their essential condition of possibility. The eye sees the eye—sees the theory of the seeing eye—through a dead eye, as is proposed by the experimental apparatus of the *Optics*:

> if, taking the eye of a newly dead person (or failing that, the eye of an ox or some other large animal), you carefully cut away the three surrounding membranes at the back . . . and put this eye in the hole of a specially made shutter. . . . Having done this, if you look at the white body you will see there, not perhaps without wonder and pleasure, a picture representing in natural perspective all the objects outside. (AT VI 115/I.166)

The living eye glued to the back of the dead eye sees what seeing is—with a troubling curiosity, as if glued to the keyhole behind which truth undresses herself—which is to see the painting of the world (in perspective, one must remember, for we will return to it). Naïve painting, that is, a native and originary painting, a first painting upon which objects accede to the authenticity of theoretical existence.

But in order to reach the *Optics*—to see sight and its painting—one will have to have gone through the method and its exposition. If the author hidden behind the picture can learn nothing from what he hears, it is because he is there to see: what this strained ear hides is the eye glued behind the picture's blind eye. Through the ear, Descartes does not learn anything, except that, since he hears voices, someone is watching him, is looking at the lifeless gaze of the portrait. This is how he sees—without seeing—and how he sees his own gaze at the very moment when he blinds his gaze by gluing it to the dark and formless reverse of the canvas that depicts his eye.

Let me repeat: This gaze does not see anything. Neither the gaze that is painted on the canvas, nor the gaze of the painter behind the canvas can see. They only seem to see. But seeming to see, or *appearing to myself as if I were seeing*, is the necessary and sufficient condition to establish the luminous evidence of the *cogito*. The Second Meditation states exactly this:

> Yet I certainly *seem* to see (*videre videor*), to hear, and to be warmed . . . and in this restricted sense of the term it is simply thinking. (AT VII 29/II.19)

> But when I see, or think I see (I am not here distinguishing the two), it is simply not possible that I who am now thinking am not something. (AT VII 33/II.22)[11]

Videor: I seem, I appear, I am seen. I appear to myself to the extent that I am seen, and I am seen as the one who seems to see. The *videor* guarantees the *cogito*, for it attests to the only presence that cannot be shaken by even the most radical doubt: *Videor* holds fast, even at the height of phantasmagoria and illusion. To seem is to create an illusion. The *videor* is the illusion that, through an unheard-of twist or perversion, anchors certainty in the deepest abyss of illusion. The place of the *videor* is indeed the painting, the portrait, the most factitious and most faithful of faces, the most blind and most clear-sighted eye.

Descartes's portrait is authentic not through its reproductive faithfulness but because, as a portrait, it only seems to see. Or more precisely, the truth function of the picture plays itself out at this strange intersection that, in the *same* place, brings about on the canvas the infinite exchange between representative values (if he seems to see, it is because he is admirably painted) and their factitious countervalues (if it is a painting, he *only* seems to see).

Integumenta

This is not all. In thus hiding himself behind his picture—and in telling a friend that he is hiding as well as dissimulating from others that he said he was hiding—Descartes imitates someone else. The hidden Descartes is himself a portrait, and one made in the likeness of a painter—or perhaps we should say in the likeness of *the* painter par excellence. In the letter to Mersenne, Descartes in fact makes use of a characteristic feature attributed to Apelles. (Consequently, by not naming Apelles, and even if Mersenne might already be familiar with the anecdote, Descartes dissimulates the fact that he follows a model: the admission of dissimulation thus involves in turn its own feint.)

What, then, is this model? It is precisely the model of painters. It is in these terms that Apelles was celebrated by all antiquity. He was the master of the portrait and—the inversion is unavoidable—the portraitist of the master since he had the exclusive privilege of executing the official portraits of Alexander.[12] Of course, Apelles owes this privilege and this mastery to his highly accomplished art of resemblance. The lifelike faithfulness (as language would have it) of Apelles's portrait was such that (as legend would have it) soothsayers (*metōposkopoi*, those who see upon the forehead, physiognomists, as the viewers of Descartes's portrait must be in order to be philosophers) were able to predict from looking at these portraits how many years were left to their originals. This striking resemblance is called *indiscreet* resemblance, (perhaps) in the mathematical sense of indiscrete, that is to say, a resemblance in which no distance from the model remains. Hence, the indiscretion of resemblance—the one that will allow the viewer to know everything about Descartes, who is laid bare as much as his truth—is the perfection of illusion. It is, strictly speaking, and as the *metōposkopoi* prove, the strictly indiscernible illusion of truth. And even though it fails to be as *true* as truth itself, it is nevertheless infinitely more than truth-like [*vraisemblable*], in that it is as operative as the truth: but operativity is perhaps exactly what grounds or forms Cartesian truth. The perfect illusion, in any case, is the *trompe-l'oeil*, in which Apelles actually excelled, for when people stood in front of his portrait of Alexander as Zeus (as God), they believed to see the hand armed with thunder (with light) springing forth from the picture toward them. Having long lived in Ephesus, Apelles is the compatriot and follower of Parrhasios, author of the famous absolute *trompe-l'oeil*: a painted veil covering a picture that thus only existed as the fiction of the irremovable veil's visible underneath. Parrhasios's non-unveilable picture governs all pictorial mimetics: Perfect resemblance is the one that cannot be removed, brushed aside, or lifted in order to exhibit the truth of its model, since it *is* this very truth—even though (or because?) it *at the same time* deceives the expectation of truth and frustrates the desire for it. Such is the case with the *Discourse*, which is very secretly placed by its author under this authority of a *glaringly truthful* resemblance.

What are the viewers of the *Discourse* seeing, then? In turns, simultaneously, they see Apelles's and Parrhasios's pictures. They see the portrait of Descartes (of Descartes's model, of the model Descartes), and they see a veil, which they are told conceals a portrait, while this painted veil in fact covers nothing. The veritable portrait is the veil itself, or the veil already pictures the portrait of which it seems to be the cover. Simultaneously, then, the viewer sees Descartes and does not see him, she will never see the true Descartes underneath a veil that cannot be lifted.

But just who is this "Descartes"? Not René Descartes, French nobleman who left for Holland and who provides in his *Discourse* a sufficient amount of detail to be recognized or at the very least suspected (it is, as we shall see later in his text, a constitutive element of the *fable* of the *Discourse* not to hide anything of the life that is depicted in it). In this respect, the anonymity of the *Discourse* is not a very difficult "portrait game" for a contemporary of the Parisian salons or schools. But the Descartes in question is the one who says *I* in this discourse, it is I insofar as I acquire the certainty of the *I* of my thinking being: it is undoubtedly this *I* that must be shown in painting, for it is his face, perhaps, that I cannot see without seeing his portrait. Descartes—the *subject* of the *Discourse*—not seeing anything, would obtain his vision by listening to the viewers who are in turn only seeing a veil, a painted veil on a gaze that feigns-to-be-painted, or a gaze painted on a model that feigns-to-be-true. Ultimately, the "true" model will always be the example of a very ancient master of illusion.

The curious structure of this anoptical labyrinth corresponds to a necessity of Cartesian science. The veil or the picture (we now understand that they are undecidably the same) is absolutely necessary. The *Regulae* have exposed the fact that the *mathesis universalis* was dissimulated by the Ancients (Cartesian authority is always ancient, and its antiquity always serves to dissimulate) only to be discovered anew by Descartes, and covered up again by him. Without the covers underneath which Descartes presents it, indeed without the *integumenta* of "ordinary mathematics," the *mathesis* would not be accessible—at least not readily—to the human mind: "I have spoken of its 'outer garment' [*integumentum*] not because I wish to conceal this science and shroud it from the gaze of the public; I wish rather to clothe and adorn it so as to make it easier to present to the human mind."[13]

We must of course both hear *and* not hear the denegation here: we must grasp the truth of the feint along with the feint of the truth. We must ask ourselves just to what extent a garment can be distinguished from a veil (or a mask), and whether or not the relation between them is precisely one of indiscreet resemblance. Adorning and dissimulating perhaps go hand in hand, and if the thing or the person can better be exposed by means of adornment, then we surmise what twisted necessity the exposition of the *mathesis* requires. As if Mathesis could only be exposed under the varnish of Mimesis.

We must also bear in mind that one of the sources of Apelles's talent was his regard for art based on arithmetic and geometry, the mathematics according to which perspective is constructed, without which there could be no pictorial illusion. Like perspective, the Cartesian *integumenta* are indispensable if one is to let *the ungraspable depth* of science *be grasped*, of this science that, at the same time, they cover. The *mathesis* is neither presented nor grasped directly. Yet it is not, for all that, reached indirectly; it cannot be a matter of making it out (under a garment that would serve the function of a negligee) or of representing it (by means of a garment that would serve the function of a mannequin). It is a matter of dressing it up in order to make it seen, because, without garments, it is not visible. The *integumentum* functions beyond or underneath the opposition between direct presentation and indirect representation. It is, if one wants, the *appresentation* of *mathesis*. The latter can only be reached by means of an interposed veil, but this veil is the mathematical adornment itself, the very position and imposition of *mathesis* by means of its interposition. For, in the end, "ordinary mathematics" is the first and purest fruit, the first existence, of *Mathesis universalis*. Thus, the varnish of mimesis is the authentic color, the veritable rose-colored blush of Mathesis. Or the reverse.

Now, according to what the *Meditations* say about painters, it is *color* that guarantees or is responsible for the truth of painting: "Or if perhaps they manage to think up something so new that nothing remotely similar has ever been seen before . . . at least the colours used in the composition must be real" (AT VII 20/II.13). Color occupies the position of certainty, which is odd if we consider that color is as such precisely without *position* and only acquires a position by being circumscribed by shape, or figure. But just as the geometrical figures of the *Regulae* function as veils that let the nudity of Science be seen, the *figure* that must be traced on the picture of the *Discourse* must serve to let the rosy blush [*l'incarnat*] of the Subject be seen. This Subject will owe his certainty only to the unde*terminable* nature of his color—indeterminable, yet *materially* certain. Its grain, its paste, its *substance* is there, spread, applied, glued to the canvas on the reverse side of which his colorless ear is glued.

Admittedly, the colors are circumscribed, otherwise they would not be there anymore; they would flow into one another, the rosy blush of the Subject would melt into . . . the ground from which it is supposed to stand out, and one would indefinitely paint grayness on the grayness of the canvas, losing both ground and figure, but they are circumscribed within the contours of "something (or some*one*?) so new that nothing remotely similar has ever been seen before." Indeed, we know that the *cogito* can neither be compared nor imitated. Descartes's figure is therefore the fruit of an "extravagant imagination" (AT IXa 15), as the translation by the Duc de Luynes says. (Foucault rebukes Derrida for using this translation instead of the Latin text, but he forgets that the Duc de Luynes was read, corrected, and approved by Descartes.) Or, if one sticks to the Latin text, it is not only "thought up" (or "invented" as Foucault translates it) but also *excogitated*, as the text says, which could not have said it better.[14] The *cogito*, insofar as it has or makes a figure, is excogitated; it is only thought by ex-posing itself, by feigning to expose itself and by exposing its feint, its fiction, its extravagance.[15]

Perspective—which is brought into play without reserve by the *trompe-l'oeil*—is the procedure whereby three dimensions may be feigned upon a surface. Perspective thus constitutes the procedure of Descartes's own exposition. In the fifth section of the *Discourse* (this treatise that the *Discourse* at once conceals and reveals, dissimulates and supplements because of its theologico-political conjuncture[16]):

> My aim was to include in it everything I thought I knew about the nature of material things before I began to write it. Now a painter cannot represent all the different sides of a solid body equally well on his flat canvas, and so he chooses one of the principal ones, sets it facing the light, and shades the others so as to make them stand out only when viewed from the perspective of the chosen side. In just the same way, fearing that I could not put everything I had in mind into my discourse, I undertook merely to expound quite fully what I understood about light. (AT VI 41–42/I.132)

Perspective is thus a necessary procedure because of a plane or flat character of discourse (planarity or platitude? Is it depth or poetry that is missing?) and what comes to collide with it: an excess of relief and of depth of thought. Of course, this traditional schema refers back to a flaw of writing. Perspective supplements the poverty of writing. It is therefore a palliative. But this palliative is remarkably successful, to the point that it does better, and perhaps more, than simply dissimulating a flaw. What Descartes sets up in the foreground and paints "facing the light" is light itself. Perspective paints the relief of light that allows us to see perspective itself. The picture paints its own exteriority and magnificently twists and diverts in this way its flat condition. The painter lets that be seen which allows to see (but has a painter even painted anything else?). In deceiving the eye of the viewer, the painter presents her with the element of her vision: the relief of light. Between the living eye and the painted eye, we no longer know which one illuminates the other—or keeps one eye on the other, in keeping with another meaning of the verb *éclairer* that was common in the seventeenth century: to watch or to spy, from behind a picture for example.

Hence, the portrait of Descartes is the portrait—striking in its resemblance—of light.

Sibi simile signum

This portrait would thus be the self-portrait par excellence, the painting before all painting of light that applies—upon which obscure canvas if not the dark reverse side of light, the blind tain of light, far more obscure and more ancient than any night—the touch of its resemblance, the touch that makes it visible.

Apelles, to whom an autobiography is also attributed, is the author of the most ancient self-portrait in the history of painting. It is Apelles whom Descartes will invoke—by name this time—when it will be a matter of explaining the origin of the idea of God within me, the second cornerstone of his doctrine. This idea, as is stated in the Third Meditation,[17] is "as it were, the mark of the craftsman stamped on his work" and he adds "not that the mark need be anything distinct from the work itself" (AT VII 51/II.35). The mark of God can therefore be myself, the thinking substance as such. It is enough to establish that this is indeed the case: "But the mere fact that God created me is a very strong basis for believing that I am somehow made in his image and likeness, and that I perceive that likeness, which includes the idea of God, by the same faculty which enables me to perceive myself" (ibid.). The proof—which, oddly enough, does not go beyond the degree of a very strong credibility—rests upon the act of creating. This can be argued in at least two ways, neither one of which excludes the other: Creation would be a degradation of the creator if it was not his reproduction; or creation necessarily introduces to the order of a second reality that of the image, but the first image cannot have any other model than the creator. The creator thus paints his self-portrait. This is what Descartes will allude to in his commentary on this passage in his *Replies to the Fifth Set of Objections*, and under the authority of Apelles: "Suppose there is a painting in which I observe so much skill that I judge that it could only have been painted by Apelles" (AT VII 372/II.256). And Descartes concludes the argument (in which the operation of God was compared simultaneously to the work of the painter and to "parental procreation"): "Again, it is not always true that there is no resemblance between the work of a craftsman and the craftsman himself, as is clear in the case of a sculptor who produces a statue resembling himself [*sibi simile signum*]" (AT VII 373/II.257).[18]

Descartes's model is thus double, and hence doubly hidden. It is Apelles, in whose image Descartes paints with a consummated art the image (the idea) of God (Alexander as God)—and it is also the self-portrait, in the image of which Descartes composes his *Discourse*—which means that he operates or creates in the image of God himself. Once more, in exposing *sibi simile signum*, Descartes declares (and dissimulates the fact that he declares): *larvatus* (as painter) *pro Deo*.

But it is not certain that the divine or the pseudo-divine author and model of the *Discourse* is simply the thinking "I," who in Descartes's soul reproduces the semblance of God. What is uncertain is not whether the portrait is that of the subject of the *Discourse* but whether this subject himself is (or is only) the luminous self-presence of his *cogito*. Perhaps the painting of light creates in turn an illusion.

The *Discourse* hides yet another feint. When in Part Five Descartes summarizes the main points of the treatise *The World*, which the *Discourse* conceals and supplements, he indicates that in the earlier treatise he proceeded not only by means of perspective but also out of prudence, by means of a fiction (which *The World* calls "fable"): "But I did not want to bring these matters too much into the open [*pour ombrager un peu toutes ces choses*]. . . . So I decided . . . to speak solely of what would happen in a new world. I therefore supposed that God now created, somewhere in imaginary spaces, enough matter . . . so as to form a chaos as confused as any the poets could invent" (AT VI 42/I.132).

An initial feint is uncovered here, that of *The World* itself: the fable of the creation of another world is but a protective rhetoric with respect to "the learned." It is really the truth of our world's laws that Descartes wants to expose. And he admits as much here when he presents his fable using the procedure of painting: "*pour ombrager*," "in order to shade."[19] But this admission deceives the eye [*trompe l'oeil*] about the dissimulation that follows. Indeed, Descartes continues: "First of all, then, I described this matter, trying to represent it so that there is absolutely nothing, I think, which is clearer and more intelligible, with the exception of what has just been said about God and the soul" (AT VI 42–43/I.132). It is exactly at this point that *The World* is most camouflaged by the *Discourse*, for the former does not deal with "what has just been said about God and the soul." In *The World*—in the feigned world of mathetic truth—the matter (i.e., the extension) of original chaos, similar to the chaos invented by poets, is the *only* thing that is most easily conceived and the conception of which is at the same time the condition for all other conceptions: "The idea of this matter is included to such an extent in all the ideas that our imagination can form that you must necessarily conceive it or else you can never imagine anything at all" (AT VI 35/I.91–92). Here, the matter of chaos is the limit of the feint of the "new World," the point at which one can no longer feign because the feint is authenticated as truth. The matter of poetic chaos proves to be the same thing (the thing itself) as the primary matter of divine creation. It thus occupies the same structural position as the *cogito*, and in the genesis of Descartes's thoughts, it is this matter that provides the *cogito* with its matrix. To the full measure that the *cogito* holds and functions as the ultimate point of a *veri*-fied feint or fiction, this matter of chaos constitutes at least its equivalent and at most its origin. Now this measure—which allows the *cogito* to hold as operation rather than as content—is far from negligible and constitutes undoubtedly the very nature and function of the *cogito*. I will not undertake its analysis here.[20] For the moment, I only ask to keep in mind, faced with Descartes's picture, that the *cogito* is preceded and as if doubled (or lined, insofar as the lining is what gives a fabric its resistance and holding, but one might also think of the theatrical sense of an actor's "body double") by the position of the elementary chaos.

Light itself comes from chaos, in the order of divine operations as well as in that of Descartes's fictioning operations (both are the same): "Let me tell you that at the moment I am busy sorting our Chaos with a view to extracting light from it."[21] The radical or even original nature of the Cartesian enterprise requires that it begin with Chaos—inseparably, indistinguishably with chaos and with the subject. The minimal condition is at once the creation of a chaos by a subject, and the conception of the subject evidenced by the matter of this chaos. One precedes the other, the other precedes the one, at the very same time. Henceforth one cannot avoid suspecting that the *cogito* itself, the *luminous* cogito, still serves as a mask for something that is strictly speaking neither soul, nor God, nor world. And one cannot avoid suspecting either that light painted in *trompe-l'oeil* can only let its relief be seen by dissimulating this obscure reverse side, the unnamable support (this *substance*) upon the chaotic grain of which it is painted. It will therefore never be possible to remove or to lift the veil or the picture, without running the risk of not seeing anything anymore, of seeing only darkness—a darkness that no light has yet separated from itself, and which does not even take the *figure* of a shadow. And yet it is also by means of the "vision" of this invisible support—*formless substance of the eye itself*—that illumination begins. Behind the picture, what does Descartes's face actually *resemble*? Behind the dead eye that deceives the eye, what does the eye (of the) subject resemble? Which *chaogito*?

Ignotus moritur sibi

If the chaogito paints itself, this means both that it *cannot* paint itself and that it cannot show itself except *in painting*. In both cases, the reason is the same: the chaogito does not resemble anything. Resemblance is required because it is impossible.

It is impossible first for the *cogito* itself. It is the subject that cannot recognize *himself*, without going through the complex apparatus whereby the *trompe-l'oeil* converts into vision the blindness of substance, of the support that can neither see nor be seen without exposing the surface of light and of the gaze. It is therefore necessary to go through the gaze of the other, which is not without danger, the danger of having the vision of oneself re-sorbed in an alienated image. Descartes later declared having adopted as his motto the following verses from Seneca, which extend the "*bene latuit*" of his first motto:

> *Illi mors gravis incubat,*
> *Qui, notus nimis omnibus,*
> *Ignotus moritur sibi.*[22]

The passage where Descartes delivers this motto is one of those—rather common, as is well known—where he declares to have henceforth resolved "to abstain from writing books." This resolution was already made at the end of the *Discourse*, and I will come back to it. Indeed, in the book—that is to say, in the picture where the subject exposes himself—what is played out is the difficulty of achieving self-vision by way of the self-portrait's false semblance, the difficulty of acceding to the face by way of the mask, to the substance by way of the surface.

This difficulty is confirmed by two characteristics of the *Discourse*, characteristics, so to speak, that frame it: It is anonymous, and it purports to be the first and last book by its author.

The anonymity of the *Discourse* does not have the function of an ordinary anonymity, unless it "unveils" the hidden workings of all anonymity. It does not simply hide its author. It hides the author that presents the picture of his own life; hence, it hides him who discovers himself in his truth. This anonymity thus declares explicitly that it is a false semblance, and in the same stroke, for lack of the author's name—and *by means of* this lack—it proclaims that *there is* an author, a unique, irreducible author, or rather an author whose unique and irreducible example will be depicted for us. It thus proclaims that the dissimulated name is the *most proper* of proper names: the name of the one who alone gave himself the method of certainty, and hence the name of the one who gives *himself* as the method of certainty and the certainty of method.[23] But the identity of this subject is valid only on the condition that it be identity *itself*, stripped completely of anything accidental or empirical (like the name René Descartes, for example) and presented in its substance as subject. Such might be, in truth, the complex reference to the author implied by the *trompe-l'oeil* in general, that is, by all painting that is subject to resemblance: there must be *no* author if the perfect illusion is to join with the very identity that (re)presents itself, and the author of such a perfect resemblance can only be the Author par excellence.[24] Anonymously, again, *larvatus pro Deo*.

On the other hand—yet confirming what has just been said—Descartes intends this anonymity as merely provisional. In this sense, it is not a mere dissimulation. It is a mask to be lifted, but it shall only be lifted once the public will have, by reading the *Discourse*, come to know its author. For the moment, the mask allows that "my work may not fall short of expectation."[25] If Descartes fears falling short with respect to what may be expected from René Descartes, it is because one should not measure the *Discourse* (the method) against its author, but rather the author against his method—that is, against the very certainty of science. Here again one must interpret the feint: under the "I might not measure up to what is expected of me," one must read: "I only measure up to the unheard-of height of what I expose." My identity is only valid as the exorbitant identity of the subject of truth: *I* think. "René Descartes" will only be revealed once he is identified with this *I* (which, as is known, identifies itself only with itself and resembles nothing).[26]

The anonymous subject of the method exposes a feigned subject in a portrait in order to find therein his truth of a subject that is impossible to feign. Without this procedure, he would never appropriate his image (his idea), but with it, he perhaps never appropriates anything but his picture.

This is undoubtedly why Descartes intends never to publish anything else. Whether it be *The World*, hidden behind the *Discourse*, or what he continued to write after it, he thought that he should "not to agree to their publication during my lifetime, so that neither the opposition and controversy they might arouse, nor the reputation they might gain for me . . . make me lose any of the time I planned to devote to my self-instruction" (AT VI 65/I.146). It is no longer a question of instructing oneself by means of the judgment of others: the gaze of the viewer, so it seems, was only necessary for the exhibition of the subject, not for the verification of science. Were he to be published, however, Descartes would expose himself to losing himself, to "dying to himself unknown," or to not knowing himself, which for the subject amounts to dying. The *exposed, excogitated* subject plays for winning his own substance at the risk of losing his own identity. Or vice versa. He will only be published posthumously, once he will have come back to himself, to this "something that has no name in any tongue."[27]

Descartes, however, continues to write. "I have come to think," he writes,

> that I must continue writing down anything I consider at all important, when I discover its truth, and that I should take as much care over these writings as I would if I intended to have them published. For this will give me all the more reason to examine them closely, as undoubtedly we always look more carefully at something we think is to be seen by others (. . . and will allow them to be read after my death). (AT VI 65–66/I.144–145)[28]

Everything happens as if writing, deficient and flat before the *Discourse*, had been discovered or had transformed itself under the cover of painting into a necessary instrument of thought. Or rather, writing itself has become painting: to write is to paint a reader in *trompe-l'oeil*. In order to "examine more closely," Descartes pictures to himself the false semblance of the other's gaze. The exhibitionist constructs the fiction of a voyeur. This is a feint, and yet it is not one: this voyeur will exist after my death, and this is where I see him. Through his own dead eye, Descartes sees the one who beholds him. He needs this extra *trompe-l'oeil* in order not to die unknown to himself.

(The author of Descartes's epitaph at St-Germain-des-Prés had understood this well:

> *Nunc veritatis quam unice coluit*
> *conspectu fruitur.*
> Now, the truth that had been his only task,
> he enjoys it through the eyes.)

Larvatus ergo

A fictive viewer is thus everywhere necessary for the exhibition of the portrait, that is, for the *conception* of the *subject* of the picture, or again, for *truth*. The truth that Cartesian mathesis erects as the certainty of the subject is at the same time determined [*décidée*] as the self-conception of this subject, or as the self-conception that this subject *is*. The ontology of subjectivity is not that of a subjective "interiority" or a consciousness; it is the ontology of the self-conception of being.

But it is the same decision that, through the exhibition of the subject, radically destroys the possibility of an apprehension-of-self. Descartes's entire discourse speaks of nothing else than self-appropriation. But its order and its position—here I have focused on the way in which this discourse gives itself as a discourse of the painting of self—conforms to the constraints of the impossibility of such an appropriation: The ontology of the *thinking substance* stands opposed in principle to the exposition of a surface covered with signs. This is what metaphysics had always said. The ontology of the *subject*, however, posits exposition itself and the production of signs as the locus and the being of substance itself. Such an ontology seeks to make the substrate visible, or rather it seeks that the substrate make *itself* visible. It is always, inevitably, the lure of its surface that it exhibits and exhibits to itself. In the very instant of the appropriation, the subject only appropriates *the abyss of a substance without surface*, or the formlessness of the substrate that has yet to take the form of a picture.[29]

For it is "true" that the surface is that which forms the ground, and that in order for the ground to see itself, it must see its surface, and that in order to see the surface, it has nothing but the gaze of others. Hence, the fiction of a viewer is also true.

"Fictive" here does not mean "imaginary" but designates a position or a *role* that is structurally indispensable in the production of the *theoretical* truth of the subject. Cartesian fiction designates the feint (it is the same word) whereby the truth of an unexhibitable identity is given, that is to say, whereby it presents and represents itself at once. This is the very feint of painting and perspective, as is explained in the *Optics*:

> You can see this in the case of engravings: consisting simply of a little ink placed here and there on a piece of paper, they represent to us forests, towns, people, and even battles and storms; and although they make us think of countless different qualities in these objects, it is only in respect of shape [*figure*] that there is any real resemblance. And even this resemblance is very imperfect, since engravings represent to us bodies of varying relief and depth on a surface which is entirely flat. Moreover, in accordance with the rules of perspective they often represent circles by ovals better than by other circles, squares by rhombuses better than by other squares, and similarly for other shapes. Thus it often happens that in order to be more perfect as an image and to represent an object better, an engraving ought not to resemble it. Now we must think of the images formed in our brain in just the same way. (AT VI 113/1.165–166)

It is clear that the "fictive" is not the "imaginary"; or rather it is, but only if the imaginary itself, the order of the image, is henceforth also the order of thought. Cartesian imagination inextricably compounds the value of irrational and dangerous "fantasy" with that of the image as the *outline* that reproduces the thing. But from the moment that the thing exists in and through its shape or figure, this outline is also *the outline that produces the thing*. Only one thing remains without figure: the thinking substance. But for any thing, and hence also for thought, there is only one law of presentation: Its figure must be outlined. It is thus the precarious articulation between the "figureless" and the law of the outline that constitutes what we call the "subject"—and initiates, through its entire history, the future privilege of the (re)presentation of space over time for Kant, with all of its consequences. Fundamentally, it is Cartesian theory that provides the true thought of the thing itself with the condition of spatial representation. And for that reason it is also the theory of the *subject*, that is, of this "homogeneity of the representational substratum," of which Panofsky speaks with regard to perspective.[30] The homogeneous substratum is the substance of a "single and immobile eye,"[31] as it is *supposed* by perspective. Descartes's philosophy finds its ground in the ontology of this *position* required by *perspective*, that is, by "clear, piercing vision." And since this position is as unassignable (being always on the reverse side of the canvas) as it is rigorously defined, this same ontology is only supported by the figuration through which one deceives the eye by painting the eye itself. The subject does not imagine himself, but since he can only be the subject of his representation, he suddenly *images himself*, he *pictures himself*.

The vision (the theory) of the subject is not "fictional." It will be better characterized by the juridical double of the word: *fictitious*. A fictitious action (*action ficticia*), in Roman law, is one in which the judge expands the validity of the law to a case to which it does not apply; yet this is a real action, and not a mere scholastic exercise. The law of Cartesian truth is the law of the vision of the subject, the law of evidence (of "natural light") that produces certainty, per-spective. The method extends its validity to the case to which it cannot apply: the subject's vision of himself, the vision of vision. Speculation is here fictitious: it thus exhibits itself not by means of mirrors, but of portraits—in other words, masks.

The eye of the mask is double. It is the painted eye on the picture, which does not see but seems to see (*videre videor*) and masks the blind eye of the painter who dissimulates himself. It is at the same time the eye of a mask, that is, the only thing in a mask that is neither feigned nor pictured. A mask does not have eyes, but holes. Behind the holes, there is the veritable eye of *one knows not whom.* The structure of the mask is thus equivalent to the structure of the face (this is why the mask deceives and pictures, deceives by picturing a figure that resembles) if the face indeed corresponds to what is expressed by Lichtenberg's aphorism reported by Freud: "He wondered how it is that cats have two holes cut in their skin precisely at the place where their eyes are."[32] But this structure is still that *of the eye itself,* which has "in the middle of it," as Descartes could not fail to note, "a small round hole, which we call the pupil, and which appears quite black in the middle of the eye, when we look at it from the outside."[33] From the outside—but we have *seen* what it means to see the pupil *from the inside*: it is just seeing, and hence not seeing vision, or it is seeing the dead eye in which one is looking. To see the living eye is always to "look at it from the outside." To see the eye is to see the mask, and this always means seeing the glaringly truthful figuration of the hole, as if this hole resounded with truth (for a mouth might open in this little hole. I will come back to this). To see the mask is to see the eye. In masking himself, Descartes has shown everything.

Let us now read the "*larvatus prodeo*" again:

> Actors, taught not to let any embarrassment show on their faces, put on a mask. I will do the same. So far, I have been a spectator in this theatre which is the world, but I am now about to mount the stage, and I come forward masked. (AT X 213/I.2)

We do not know where Descartes got the idea of attributing to the theatrical mask a modest or bashful function, whether this explanation is traditional or whether it is Descartes's invention.[34] Embarrassed by what to make of this passage, Adam and Tannery affirm that it must involve a recollection of theater from college: Only young amateur actors have to hide their embarrassment about appearing on stage. This is not very convincing, as one can see . . . On the other hand, it is possible to wonder in which plays Descartes could have had the occasion to act in La Flèche: *Les fausses vérités ou Croire ce qu'on ne voit pas et ne pas croire ce qu'on voit* [False Truths, or To Believe What One Does Not See and Not Believe What One Sees] by d'Ouville, *l'Innocente infidélité* [Innocent Infidelity] by Rotrou, *la Fidèle tromperie* [Faithful Deceit] by Gougenot, *les Apparences trompeuses* [Deceptive Appearances] by Boisrobert, or *He Who Is Similar to Himself* by de Alarcón?

Did Descartes, in the guise of Lidias, one of the doppelgängers of *la Ressemblance* by Rotrou, declaim the verse: "I believe myself to have a mask"? Or as one of the two Dromion in *la Comédie des erreurs*: "I am to myself disguised"?[35] Is the *Discourse on the Method* not the theory of baroque aesthetics, of tragicomedy in *trompe-l'oeil* style (plot and decor) that becomes widespread during the very period when Descartes is writing the *Discourse*? Descartes's thinking indeed exemplifies *baroque thinking* par excellence, that is to say, in the end, and as I think can now be "seen," it is less a theory *of* the *trompe-l'oeil* than the *theory in trompe-l'oeil*, with everything that this expression might entail . . .

. . . or rather, with everything that this expression might not succeed in saying without collapsing upon itself.

In any case, one knows that Descartes had written three acts of a comedy, which according to Baillet "was just like a pastoral fable"[36] (it is the first form of tragicomedy, an edifying fable the mechanisms of which are masks, false pretenses, metamorphoses). Again according to Baillet, in this play Descartes "wanted to cloak the love of wisdom, the search for truth and the study of philosophy with the figurative discourse of his characters."[37] We will never know exactly what these masks were like. I know with all certainty, however, that in this scenography (it is the ancient word for the science of perspective), *I* was staging, from beginning to end, a viewer, myself, whom I never saw and always took for another, that is, for myself. Leibniz kept for us a partial description of this incomplete Fable.[38] The heroine, Parthenia, learns that she is a princess, she "speaks to herself about it and deliberates whether she ought to love Alixan," who is also a prince, but unbeknownst to him. Alixan, from a hiding place, hears this monologue, and then reveals himself. Leibniz is astonished by this scene, which is contrary to the common practices according to which the lovers only discover their true identity late in the play. Leibniz is thinking of the dramatic turn of events in classical theater. Descartes does not know revelation in this sense: He stages him who *steals* from the truth—from Parthenia, the virgin—the secret of her identity, and of her love for him, prince unknown to himself and who listens to her while remaining hidden.

But let us return to the mask. It does not so much hide the subject as much as his shame. This means just as well that it shows the subject, that it allows him to show himself relieved of all shame. The mask hides and shows at the same time the shamelessness of the subject that exposes himself, the "blush of the face" that according to Ferenczi is equivalent to an erection.[39] The portrait of Descartes that no one has ever seen, which is however his only portrait, is that of an erect Descartes.

But just as well—by a trick of Medusa, as unavoidable here as elsewhere— this portrait is also that of Descartes's *confusion*. If there cannot be a subject except an erect one, this very erection plunges him into confusion. The mask dissimulates the subject in disarray, in ruin, ashamed of himself and bereft of assurance at the moment where he presents himself. But since the subject *was* not before appearing on the stage where he will say: "I am," the mask also dissimulates the confusion in which the subject comes to himself (and hence comes into being), obscure as he is to himself beneath the dark underside of the mask, becoming indistinguishable from this other whose role he plays in order to appear to himself.

There is no one behind the mask: Thought has no figure or shape, if "by a body I understand whatever has a determinable shape."[40] There is someone beneath the mask, since "he" comes forward masked. There is someone who might well be no one, since "he" resembles nothing; someone who is indistinguishable from anyone, from any *person* [personne], that is to say, in Latin, as is well known, from the role or the mask with which "he" covers his shame.[41]

But this modesty is the condition of the knowledge of the subject. The text of the "Preliminaries" adds: "Science is like a woman: if she stays faithful to her husband she is respected; if she becomes common property she grows to be despised" (AT X 214/I.2). *Bene latuit*: behind the mask, science will remain by her husband—Descartes. Or Descartes, masked woman, remains by God. In this intimacy of the mask's underside, shame could very well be abolished. Truth could lay itself bare: "The sciences are at present masked, but if the masks were taken off, they would be revealed in all their beauty" (AT X 215/I.3).

This is still in the same text, and like a singular way of throwing off the mask. Descartes and the sciences, or God and Descartes—in short, the subject and himself—naked, could *conceive (of) the subject in all purity*. But this is perhaps what is not possible, or at least never visible. Descartes's children, the little Francine and the *ego* of the *cogito*, always remained hidden and died in their youth.

Larvatus pro Deo: in all initiations, in all sacred rituals, the sole function of masks has always been to hide an individual *who was never one*, who ceases to be one at the very moment when he masks himself; in his place, the mask exhibits the figure of a god, never visible without a mask. Descartes's subject is initiated into the theory of the Subject by putting forward: *larvatus ergo sum*. "The Cogito doesn't mean anything in its own terms. It signifies only as mimicry,"[42] writes Valéry. And Alain: "Man finds himself to be everything, and the reader loses himself. This black gaze does not promise anymore."[43]

Mundus Est Fabula

"The apologue consists of two parts, one of which might be called its body, the other its soul. Its body is the fable; its soul the moral."[1] So says La Fontaine in the Preface to his *Fables*. This doctrine appears unmistakably Cartesian. But it is Cartesian to a greater degree and in a different way than one suspects. The soul for Descartes—or more precisely, and provisionally,[2] the human soul considered in its substantial qualification as the *thinking* soul—proposes and exposes itself as the morality of a fable. This does not take place for reasons of convenience, expediency, or literary ornamentation, but by virtue of a fundamental necessity of the *cogito*. This fable itself is the story of Descartes's thinking life, his intellectual autobiography. Such an autobiography in turn can obey no other logic than that of the invention of its own fable. The structure and function of the *cogito* are subjected through and through to the fabulatory law. This is what must be demonstrated.

65

Let us place as the frontispiece one of the portraits of Descartes, the one painted by J.-B. Weenix around 1647. It is not necessary to show the image here since it is a portrait that must be *read*. René Descartes is shown holding an open book, the left page of which is visible. Written upon it is: *mundus est fabula*. That is to say, according to the Latin as well as the modern acceptation, both "the world is a theater play" and "the world is a fable," respectively. Some traditions trace the origin of this maxim—at least insofar as the comparison of the world to a theater is concerned—as far back as Pythagoras. Thus, as far back as the origin itself (of philosophy). According to this emblematic portrait, Descartes's entire doctrine consists in a reinscription of this age-old maxim. What if philosophy as a whole indeed began again with Descartes through the repetition of this formula, a formula that from now on would acquire the status both of science and of the subject?

This is not a hypothesis: With Descartes, *mundus est fabula* indeed becomes the formula of the science of the world. And since this science is such only through what, in the first instance, constitutes it as a science of the subject—science that the subject possesses, but also science that he has of himself (science that he possesses only through and according to his self-knowledge)—the formula becomes that of the ontology of subjectivity, that is, again, of the *terra firma* or the "solid ground"[3] that, according to Hegel, metaphysics reaches with Descartes, a solid ground upon which we always walk, especially when we walk on the moon, and upon which we continue to build our cities, our states, our factories. We have settled upon the solid ground of the subject. But the subject is the one who has a *world*: something that is at *his* disposal, something that is ready to be used by him, that is *proper* to him, that is well disposed to being his property. Today, after Descartes, the subject is the world, and vice versa. The maxim must also be taken to mean: *mundus*—the one that is pure, proper—*est fabula*. The Subject, the pure belonging to self of the Self, is a fable.

This is no wordplay: It is the same word, *mundus*, pure, clean, proper, well-disposed, well-ordered, world. This is what, according to Plutarch, Pythagoras meant by the word *kosmos*: The world is a nice arrangement, clear, clean, pure, and proper. The world is that which is not impure [*immonde*].[4]

Thus we must demonstrate the following: what is not impure, what is world absolutely, what disposes itself from out of itself in its self-property— is a fable, or rather, it is the Fable.

Not that we mean this in the everyday sense of "it's merely a fable." Maybe the painter Weenix understood the expression he was painting (who chose it? the painter or the model?) in the most banal, most proverbial sense, a sense that was quite commonplace in Baroque thought: the world we see and in which we live has no more reality than the illusion of a fable offered to us in a theater. Descartes most likely agrees with this; he is also part of the Baroque banality. He even provides the theory of the irreality of the world we know. Thus begins *The World*:

> The subject I propose to deal with in this treatise is light, and the first point I want to draw to your attention is that there may be a difference between the sensation we have of light (i.e. the idea of light which is formed in our imagination by the mediation of our eyes) and what it is in the objects that produces this sensation within us (i.e. what it is in a flame or the sun that we call by the name "light"). (AT XI 3/I.81)

The proper aim of the Cartesian enterprise will nevertheless be to pierce the illusion and to establish the kind of *truth* that the subject has at his disposal even though this same subject might not know the things themselves: *certainty*. This has nothing to do with the subjectivism according to which "mundus est fabula" is understood by everyone around Descartes. The doctrine of ideas in the *Meditations* will be, on the contrary, the doctrine of the resemblance of ideas, which are "like pictures" (AT VII 42(IXa 33)/ II.29), to their originals. But this resemblance is less the effect of an imitation, which would still leave us in a theater, than of a communication of being through a causation that produces the idea: "But in order for a given idea to contain such and such objective reality, it must surely derive it from some cause which contains at least as much formal reality as there is objective reality in the idea"[5] (AT VII 41/II.28–29). Thus, even though I cannot know everything, or know everything perfectly, "it is certain . . . that I have in me the means of knowing with certainty" everything in the world.[6]

Cartesian knowledge is the obliteration of the subjectivism that takes the world to be a mere fable. In this regard, the portrait painted by Weenix is a gross error.

But Cartesian knowledge shatters subjectivism only because the Subject of this knowledge, the proprietor of certainty, wins himself over and exposes himself only by presenting his own veritable fable. This fable is the *Discourse on the Method*.

> My present aim, then, is not to teach the method which everyone must follow in order to direct his reason correctly, but only to reveal how I have tried to direct my own. One who presumes to give precepts must think himself more skilful than those to whom he gives them; and if he makes the slightest mistake, he may be blamed. But I am presenting this work only as a history or, if you prefer, a fable in which, among certain examples worthy of imitation, you will perhaps also find many others that it would be right not to follow; and so I hope it will be useful for some without being harmful to any, and that everyone will be grateful to me for my frankness.
> (AT VI 4/I.112)

Descartes presents [*propose*] his Discourse *as a fable*. This is not a comparison; his text does not borrow, by imitating it, the appearance of a literary genre. Rather it is given *as* a fable, and it must be used *as* a fable. Hence, the fable does not present the motif of a fiction that would be essentially opposed to the truth, but would come to serve as its instrument or its ornament. If here the fable must introduce some *fiction*, it will be by virtue of a completely different procedure: it will not bestow fiction "upon" truth, or beside it, but will introduce fiction *into* it.

From the outset, the "fable" of the *Discourse* exceeds, then, the theme of fiction, and maybe even completely turns it back on itself. In truth, so to speak, it will henceforth only be a matter of the way in which a certain reversal of fiction is the operator of the truth of the subject.

This is why the prefatory position of the fable in the *Discourse* is only distantly related to what could be called the *literary* contrivances of fiction, which are used by Descartes in many of his other texts: for example, when he invites the reader of the *Principles* to thumb "quickly through the whole book like a novel" (AT IXb 11/I.185); or when he sets up such literary contrivance expressly as part of a staging method, for example in the unfinished dialogue that is called *The Search for Truth*; or again, as in the comedy or "pastoral fable," the text of which has been lost, when he wants to write a literary work with philosophical content.[7] In all of these cases—the frequency of which, moreover, cannot fail to alert us to Descartes's unexpected insistence on these literary devices, which were for that matter quite common in his time—it is a matter of the fable insofar as we should not believe in it, the kind of fable that is mentioned in the twelfth of the *Regulae* so that it can be compared to the illusions of the senses, this fable that is not a "true story," a *res gesta*.[8]

Before the *Discourse*, however, the same motif of the fable had appeared and played a different role in *The World*. When Descartes moves to the description of the elementary structure and matter of the world as he wants to know it—let us say, when he moves to the description of the scientific truth of the world—he states (at the end of Chapter 5): "But in order to make this long discourse less boring for you, I want to clothe part of it in the guise of a fable, in the course of which I hope the truth will not fail to become sufficiently clear, and will be no less pleasing to see than if I were to set it forth wholly naked" (AT XI 31/I.90). According to this presentation, the fable of the World is a "covering" intended to please. One should take a closer look, however. Descartes mentions the risk that the fable veils the truth a bit too much. Yet, since the *Regulae*, the truth of Cartesian science, is precisely such that it *requires* a garment (that of ordinary mathematics[9]) in order to show itself. This primary function, which exceeds in principle that of a literary ornament, is further complicated in *The World*. The fable in question (or the *feint*, as it will be called later) will be that of God creating a new world. Or more precisely, it will be, *at the same time*, Descartes's invention of a new world ("which I shall bring into being . . . in imaginary spaces"), God's creation of a new world ("let us suppose that God creates anew"), and the repetition of the creation of our world (we must go back beyond the "five or six thousand years" that mark the age of the earth).[10] We have, then, a fiction the purpose of which is to expose the truth of this world through the explanation of its constitution. But this is only possible if the fiction is intrinsically related to the explication and enters in relation with it through its own invention of fiction. It is not a matter of presenting "the things which are in fact in the real world," but of "mak[ing] up [*feindre*], as I please, a world . . . which nevertheless could be created exactly as I have imagined it [*aurai feint*]" (AT XI 36/I.92).[11] The fable of the World is then less the instrument of an exposition than *the organ of an equivalent of creation*, and of an equivalent creation (equivalent to *the* Creation). In *inventing* this fable, I make—I make and I feign, I fiction, I fashion—a world. This world might not be the actual world, but it does not contravene the laws of effective creation. Hence, it can be the learned truth of this world.

It is therefore not a matter of providing a fictive yet realistic equivalent to the real world for Descartes: Such verisimilitude could be established only on a prior knowledge of the "true" world. Rather, what must be provided is the true invention of a world. For if the world of fiction and the world of reality are not identical, the activities of invention and of creation are on the other hand identical—and they yield Descartes's very identity. The one world is not the veri-similitude of the other: Both are the same inaugural truth. The inventor of the fable is the God of a world that, even though it is not the world itself, is nevertheless *another true world*, and is so *because it is invented*, and hence answers to the conditions of a possible creation.[12] The subject of true knowledge must be the inventor of his own fable.

The *Discourse* radicalizes this exigency and pushes it to the point of ontology.

The *fable* of the Discourse no longer has anything of a literary ornament. It has even stripped itself of the fiction or feint of being a simple ornament, with which the fable of *The World* still clothed itself. It is the ordering according to which the *Discourse* is proposed. The text therefore leaves no doubt as to how one ought to understand the term "fable": "I am presenting this work only as . . . a fable in which, among certain examples worthy of imitation" (AT VI 4/I.112). Here it is a matter of the fable as moral genre, of the fable insofar as it teaches or delivers a "morality." What here properly makes up the fable is its exemplary story.

The literary theory of the fable entailed by the *Discourse* is the one that will be developed after Descartes (to what extend should we say: because of him?) by classical poetics:

> THE first thing we are to begin with for Composing a *Fable*, is to chuse the Instruction, and the point of Morality, which is to serve as its Foundation, according to the Design and End we propose to our selves. . . .

> In the next place this *Moral Truth* must be reduc'd into Action, and a general Action must be feign'd in Imitation of the true and singular Actions. [This is the moment of the invention of the fable; the fable must disguise "the point of Morality," the instruction must remain hidden.] . . .

> The Names that are given to the Personages do first specify a *"Fable."* (Book I, Chapter VII)

> That the *Epick Poem* is a *Fable;* that is, not the *Rehearsal* of the *Action* of some one *Hero,* in order to form Mens Manners by his Example; but, on the contrary, a Discourse invented to form the Manners by the *Recital* of a *feign'd Action,* and describ'd at pleasure under the borrow'd Name of some Illustrious Person or other, that is made choice of, after the *Platform* of the Action, that is ascrib'd to him, is laid. (Book I, Chapter XIV)[13]

Let us assume for the moment that the reader of the *Discourse* cannot but appeal to this conception of the fable. "Discourse on the Method" rigorously means, then, "Fable on the Method."

But one also notices immediately in what way Descartes's poetics differs from literary poetics. First, his character is anonymous, and hence his fable is not "specified." It is Fable *in genere,* general Fable, Fable that generates every fable and hence every discourse.

On the other hand, and as if inversely, the "general action" that the fable will propose is not "feigned in imitation of" a "singular action." It is nothing but the singular action of the author, who is in turn the (anonymous) character. The Discourse is the Fable of the generality of a singular and veritable action. It thus proposes a veridical story, and the choice of the "point of Morality" in its composition blends completely with the "reduction of this moral truth into Action." In other words, all the compositional operations of the fable are cancelled or reduced to a "moment of invention," which itself strictly merges with the simple decision to declare what I have lived through. What we are given to read is the discourse of truth in act, the discourse of Truth's action.

We are not at all dealing with a fable, and this poetics is precisely the opposite to that of the poem. Why then "present this work as a fable"? This is the question that we must slowly, patiently answer in accordance with the order of action of the *Discourse* itself.

Indeed, the commentaries on Descartes's proposal that may be made independently of the *Discourse*—that is, independently of the *philosophy* of the Discourse—can lead only to dead ends. Such is the case with most of the classic readings of Descartes when, as rarely happens, they at least point out and attempt to interpret this proposal (that is, to treat it otherwise than as a pure and simple staging ornament).[14]

For instance, we might note that the fable as an instructive narrative is situated halfway between a moral theory proper and a simple narration. But then we find ourselves definitely incapable of understanding how this intermediary form can be suitable for the account of a method that gives itself as nothing other than the method of truth in the sciences. We are henceforth condemned to going back and forth between a series of hypotheses, each one as untenable as any other: Either we consider the *Discourse* as a preliminary step before the metaphysical account proper of the *Meditations* (but such a conception, which proves unacceptable as soon as one turns to the texts themselves, prevents us in any case from asking why this preliminary step imposed itself on Descartes, and why the definitive step of the *Meditations* also takes the form of a narrative). Or we must conclude that this method claims to propose itself only for René Descartes and for nobody else, and we will see how the *Discourse* strictly refutes such a hypothesis, or we must give up on the motif of the moralizing fable and come back to a conception of literary garment: A feigned story would come to clothe a universal truth.

Yet, this last hypothesis also unsettles the classic interpretation, which must then wonder whether the *Discourse*'s intellectual autobiography is fictive or not. In order to acknowledge the authenticity of the *cogito* (and it must be acknowledged, even if its universal validity can be put into question, or else the *Discourse* can only be considered as a joke), this interpretation must claim that this autobiography is not, on the whole, fictive. However, this does not affect in any way the question of its metaphysical status . . . But it would be of no help to hold on to the opposite thesis and to claim (as we would undoubtedly be ready to do today) that this autobiography is but a fiction. In both cases, the motif of the fable as Descartes puts it into play becomes contradictory, even absurd.

The fable of the *Discourse* cannot be treated as a literary garment, and neither can it be questioned in terms of its truth-relation to an experience external to the Discourse itself. The question of the fable of the Discourse, of the Fable-Discourse, cannot be approached through the distinction between truth and fiction. This distinction, which Descartes also employs (it is tempting to say, like everyone else in the world, that is, to the extent that he inherits it from the philosophical tradition as a whole), can only have a secondary and derivative status with regard to the founding gesture of the *Discourse*. This is one of the conclusions that will have to be drawn once we have approached the Fable through the only remaining path: that of the Discourse itself.[15]

Why a fable? The first answer is provided by Descartes at the same time as the proposal itself. Although the fable is defined as a story that furnishes examples, not all of the examples in such a story are necessarily worthy of imitation. This grants to this fable a quite peculiar status. Either we must call *example* only that which (or the figure that) in a fable carries its morality, and no fable could comprise more than one example (more than one truth, more than the inevitably unique truth) or all the figures of the fable must be called "examples." But then we must:

1. understand the possibility that several figures be included within the single character of this fable,[16] and
2. understand—above all—why it is that, unlike any other fable, this fable does not point out in and of itself what the *right* example is . . .

In a fable, the narrative must lead to the same point as the discourse, the "hidden instruction" must be identified with and by a character. But here everything contributes to blur this schema: there is only one character, and he is not entirely exemplary. We will see that the remainder of the narrative does not shed any further light on the eventual division between what is imitable and what is not.

Nevertheless, the proposal of the fable *also* contains the instructive decision that we expect. Indeed, Descartes says: I present this story only as a fable, for I do not give any absolute "precepts," since this would imply that I possess an authority superior to ordinary men. I have nothing else to communicate than the path I have followed. I do not teach (which invalidates the function of the fable as defined by the adage *fabula docet*), I only *show or make visible* [fais voir]. What can be made visible when one does not teach is oneself. There is no "hidden instruction" here, but the instruction itself, the motif or intention of instructing is as if withdrawn from the fable. Here, authority, truth as authority, *withdraws itself* [se retranche]. And it is in this way that the fable teaches, *fabula docet*. I teach first and foremost that I am not teaching.

It is therefore necessary to reverse anew the reversal of the poem that seemed to us to make up the poetic of the *Discourse*. Here the "discourse" is withdrawn from the "narrative." *The discourse withdraws itself* might be the still enigmatic formula of this Discourse.

Only the narrative remains, in which the function of exemplarity is blurred or undecided. *Autobiography* is the necessary genre of whoever renounces all teaching authority (renounces all truth that is taught from a position of authority and hence that is taught period, that is, all truth that comes to a "subject" from the outside), but who does not for all that renounce all presentation of an example: that is to say, does not renounce presenting something that can be imitated, and hence some *originality*, in every sense of the term. Or, more precisely, the autobiographical gesture in general— and even those that would not give anything to imitate, either by excess or lack of "originality" in the common sense—cannot by definition be conceived of in any other way than as the gesture of originality.

Our difficulty then lies in bringing to light *the original of the Discourse*: what it proposes for imitation, what distinguishes this discourse from any other, but also the one who writes it. And the originality of this original certainly lies in the fact that in this fable, it is the narrative that makes up the discourse.

The narrative of my life becomes discourse. The point of morality lies in the fact that I recount, quite simply and plainly, the path that I have followed, without taking care to separate the more from the less recommendable. This is indeed how the originality of the fable becomes immediately apparent to us: It resides in what "everybody will be grateful" to the author for, it resides in its *frankness.* The question here is not that of a division between more or less good examples: There is essentially only one exemplarity of the *Discourse*, one morality of the fable, which is frankness. It is through this frankness that Descartes distinguishes himself from all the makers of doctrines and precepts. Because he presents no teaching of truth, his work must be taken as a fable: and herein lies its whole lesson. Just as La Fontaine's *The Wolf and the Lamb,* for example, is the fable of the right of the strongest, the Discourse is the *fable of frankness.*

The Discourse is not the fable of frankness in the sense that its instruction would argue in favor of the moral virtue of frankness, for such a fable would amount to hiding the lesson that establishes the value of this virtue under the disguise of some example. But here, the value of frankness is obviously presupposed. It goes without saying that nothing is more worthy of esteem than a frank work [*écrit franc*] (that reports everything about the biography in question), and a free writing [*franc-écrit*][17]—that is, a discourse, because it reports everything, that *frees itself from the fabulatory condition of doctrinal and authoritative discourses.*

The advantage—or the exemplarity—of the fable has nothing to do with a moral; rather it lies in this "morality." The only discourse of truth is the discourse that is freed from the affabulations of those who "think [themselves] more skilful" (AT VI 4/I.112). The presupposition of the moral value of frankness allows for the *gnoseological* "morality" of this fable. The emancipation [*affranchissement*] of the fable constitutes all the instruction (at once hidden and revealed, as we see) of the fable of frankness: the advantage is truth *itself.*

This theoretical morality is indeed the one that will be drawn from the whole autobiography that begins immediately after ("From my childhood I have been nourished upon letters") and that will be drawn in particular from an entire critique of *fables* and *examples*.

In the first part of the *Discourse*, fabulation and exemplarity comprise the recurring motif of Descartes's denunciation of the education he received in school as well as from books and from "the great book of the world" (AT VI 9/I.115). In the end, Descartes will have resolved "to undertake studies within myself" (AT VI 10/I.116) and to "construct [my thoughts] upon a foundation which is all my own" (AT VI 15/I.118). The reason is that, in books and in the world, in the examples they contain and in the examples that they are, he will have encountered almost exclusively "extravagances."

But what is extravagance? Fables provide us with its model and structure:

> Moreover, fables make us imagine many events as possible when they are not. And even the most accurate histories, while not altering or exaggerating the importance of matters to make them more worthy of being read, at any rate almost always omit the baser and less notable events; as a result, the other events appear in a false light, and those who regulate their conduct by examples drawn from these works are liable to fall into the excesses [*extravagances*] of the knights-errant in our tales of chivalry, and conceive plans beyond their powers. (AT VI 6–7/I.114)[18]

The extravagance of fables is thus defined precisely by the omission of what the fable of the *Discourse* does not omit. The Discourse reports everything: The fable of frankness is a frank fable. It is more faithful than "the most accurate stories"—it is veridical.

This fable is therefore not only the opposite of fables: It is also, as we can see, their perfection, if indeed it is the *fable of fidelity*, in the sense that its narrative (or its feint) is absolutely and rigorously faithful to its discourse (to its veracity, which hence is veracity *itself*). It is that toward which all fables tend without ever reaching it (why? this is what Descartes does not say; it is what all fables lack *as a matter of principle*, all but one: this Discourse). This fable is the original of all fables, upon which all fables should be modeled. It is the fabulous example of the veritable fable, of the true fable.

Hence, we must understand that the "knights-errant in our tales of chivalry" are bad examples, not because they are excessive but because they are lacking. They are not true enough, that is to say, they do not succeed in showing *everything*. And showing everything, not hiding anything, is an endeavor that surpasses the prowess of these knights-errant—or rather, those attributed to them by their authors. But no knight-errant will ever be able to show everything unless he is himself the author, unless he invents himself. The one who says "I" here is the knight-errant of an infinitely more modest and infinitely more illustrious adventure: the fabulous truth of the one who recounts himself. But clearly not in the name of the empirical singularity of a life among others (the modern value of *sincerity* will only ever be a psychological and literary by-product of the ontology that is articulated here), for the narrative henceforth would not be a discourse, that is, a fable. But here we are faced with the case—exceptional, unique—where *there is discourse only when there is nothing left but the narrative.*

This is why it can only be a matter of the life, exemplary as a matter of principle, of the one who is of himself *the* truth, and not of the one who exhibits *his* truth; but not, however, of the one who would be the truth in order to be "more skillful" than the others. It is a matter of the life of the one who is the truth insofar as he is frankly himself.[19] Undoubtedly, this implies in the end that it must be a matter of the truth insofar as it is to itself the story (the veridical narrative) of its life, its own *res gesta*. The Discourse is the gest of truth: the Absolute Novel (*absolute* meaning, above all: emancipated and absolved from any affabulation).

It follows inevitably that if knights-errant should not be imitated, the example of Descartes, for its part, is *inimitable* (which ends up completely obscuring—or elucidating—the distinction between examples that can be recommended and the other examples in the *Discourse*):

> If I am sufficiently pleased with my work to present you with this sample of it
> [*le modèle*], this does not mean that I would advise anyone to imitate it. Those
> on whom God has bestowed more of his favours will perhaps have higher aims;
> but I fear that even my aim may be too bold for many people. The simple
> resolution to abandon all the opinions one has hitherto accepted is not an
> example that everyone ought to follow. The world is largely composed of two
> types of minds for whom it is quite unsuitable. (AT VI 15/I.118)[20]

The model withdraws—it withdraws into its original. What I show you or let you see does not constitute a *model*. If it did, it would have to be some narrative feigned in order that my discourse be understood. But it is my discourse itself that I let you see in the pure identity of its narrative.

Mundus, the pure, the all-to-itself and the well-ordered-in-itself—*ego*—*est fabula*: I am fabulous, and even less than any knight-errant can become an example.

The reason for this is not that my example is even more extravagant. Or it is because my example functions according to the logic of a passage to the limit that is constantly at work here. What is fabulously inimitable is to renounce all fables and all examples and to hold *oneself* in this destitute simplicity, set up as a model that can no longer serve as an example *since, in order to imitate it, one has to start by not believing in it anymore*. The Discourse can be neither taught nor believed. Its own communication passes to the limit.

In the *Discourse*, narrative, discourse, and fable all pass together to the limit, in their own limit. They are accomplished by means of their withdrawal. The passage to the limit of extravagance no longer extravagates, no longer goes beyond the *subject* of the fable. The passage to the limit of the example is what cannot be imitated; it is the original—an original that anyone can produce (perhaps), but that no one can reproduce. Such is the *cogito*—that is (ultimately) the content of this story.

The *cogito* resists extravagance: "And observing that this truth *'I am thinking, therefore I exist'* was so firm and sure that all the most extravagant suppositions of the sceptics were incapable of shaking it, I decided that I could accept it without scruple as the first principle of the philosophy I was seeking" (AT VI 32/I.127). This is a matter neither of a chance encounter of words nor of a distant analogy between the *cogito* and the fable. In accordance with everything that precedes, the *cogito* (which is the fable's "instruction" and "action," its instructive action and its active instruction) has the exact structure of the fable that exposes it.

The demonstrative procedure of the *cogito*—which should rather be called *monstrative*, since we know that Descartes will later specify that it does not require "the kind of knowledge that is acquired by means of demonstrations"[21]—is familiar enough that we can immediately draw out its decisive point: If the cogito is unshakable, it is because it forms the point where I can no longer feign, *the point of the impossible feint or fiction*, or else the point of the feint's passage to its limit.

Initially, we can recognize, at least formally, the very position of the Fable-Discourse: the extreme point, exceeding all novels and all treatises, *where "something" withdraws itself in truth.*

This correspondence is not formal, however. The only *content* of the cogito is to be this point. It is not found *at* the extremity of the feint, as if it were its absolute exteriority of truth; rather it *is* this extremity *itself.* The height of feint—or of fiction, since they are the same word and have the same function, that of the Fable, beginning with *The World*—is that *I am feigning.*

Thus, the *extremity* constitutes, in all respects, the position and the nature of the *cogito. Extremum* is the superlative of *exterum:* The extremity is that which is most exterior. It is, of all the things that are interior, the one that is farthest out. In all extremity, not only do the interior, the inside, or the property of a being reach their limit, the ultimate point of their completion and of their closure, but they also exceed this closure and undo their own completion. Extremity of discourse, extremity of narrative, extremity of fable and truth: all these extremities constitute only one extremity, not because they would be put together by addition, composition, or synthesis; on the contrary, they make (and unmake) "one," because each is an excess that passes into the other, so that none returns to the same. Therefore, their unity—the unity of discourse, narrative, fiction, and truth—becomes in its turn an extremity (this eludes all forms of thinking that, in one way or another, *identify* fiction and truth). It is the extreme extremity of the *cogito.* Hence, *cogito* is that which, in this extremity, is extreme. *Cogito* is *the extremity* itself, provided that from now on we understand this word as a quality and not as a position, that is to say, provided we understand it in the same register as "substantiality," for example. And the substantiality of the cogito is finally nothing other than its extremity.

As we already have to say, the *cogito* is not only *excogitate* (after Descartes, and before him, the word *excogité* was part of the French language). It is itself the excogitation, the simultaneous height of thought and extravagance, of the direct discourse of truth and the unheard-of machination of a fabulous narrative.

That substantiality, in general or absolutely, is an extremity is undoubtedly what metaphysics, since it has come to an end, does not cease to teach us in spite of itself. It is from the question concerning essence "as the *question* of essence" that the necessity arises to observe (as far as it is a matter of "observing" anything) that "the essence finds itself as it were with-drawn *by* its own disenclosure," and this even within, or starting from, the Aristotelian problematic of "substance."[22] But it is only when substantiality accomplishes itself as subjectivity that this "with-drawal" [*re-trait*] of essence manifests itself truly as such, for the extremity of the Cartesian Subject, his extreme *nature*, strips him once and for all of any property of "principle," "ground," "last foundation," and instead of "positing" him, only *ex-poses* him as the becoming-extreme of extremity. Or more exactly, it is only thanks to this extremization, this (narrative/discursive, veridical/fabulous) ex-position or extra-position, and in its reflux in a sense, that the Subject can acquire or recapture his position as ground, but as a ground that from now on will necessarily be affected by its own extremity.

This extremization is made possible only by methodic doubt, but *methodic* doubt is nothing else than the deliberate progression of the Subject toward its own extremity. This extremity is the point from which it is possible to doubt, that is, to feign and to doubt everything, which is also to feign that there is nothing at all: it is the extreme feint. On this extremity, this feint exceeds itself in truth, in this truth that says there is that—*ego*—which feigns. But the very truth of this truth—the extreme truth—consists in the movement and the structure of the extremization as such: the putting-outside-of-himself of the Subject who ex-poses himself in this way, or else the withdrawal to which his extremity compels him in regard to his very truth. *The truth as subject can only withdraw itself from itself,* and this is why "I am frank" could only be exposed by means of "I am feigning."

Descartes does not write, "I am feigning." Not really. He immediately substitutes, or has always already substituted, "I think." Rigorously, this *thought* is nothing other than the *feint*: "But immediately I noticed that while I was trying thus to think everything false, it was necessary that I, who was thinking this, was something" (AT VI 32/I.127). What does *being* mean here—or *something*? It is obviously the subject of fiction, the sub-stance that supports it and engenders it. In order to feign one must think, and in order to think one must be. However, this cannot be demonstrated. It cannot be demonstrated because it is truly a matter neither of a logical consecution nor of an ontological subordination. Or rather, what can only be exposed in the form of a logical consecution ("it was necessary that . . .") is actually given through an immediate apprehension and requires no operation of thought. Being as thought is not given by a thought but through "that internal awareness which always precedes reflective knowledge. This inner awareness of one's thought and existence is so innate in all men that, although we may pretend that we do not have it if we are overwhelmed by preconceived opinions and pay more attention to words than to their meanings, we cannot in fact fail to have it" (AT VII 422/II.285).[23]

However well I might feign, I cannot at this farthest point of the feint not know that I am. And all my fictions will only increase the certitude of this being, for fiction is in effect nothing (aside from the fact that here it is a fiction that nothing exists) if not that I fiction: I think. Therefore I exist, but this "therefore" is nothing other than a kind of "inner awareness" that is always-already given at the very opening (or closing) of my fiction: I feign, I *am* feigning.

Premise or substance (being) are contemporaneous with consequence or accident (thought) in the same way as *lux* et *lumen* are contemporaneous.[24] What is reached here in the double light of fiction is this luminous contemporaneity; it is therefore less the light, luminous matter, or lighting of a thing, than that which sheds light or enlightens (and as we know, will shed light on all things): What is reached here is *illumination*.

At this very extremity where the feint blinds itself (in the fiction of not seeing any world), *the feint illuminates itself*. This does not mean that it is brought to light, revealed as feint and condemned. It does not melt like the wax of a fiction in the sun of truth. It illuminates itself as being my fiction, and thus illuminates itself as *being*. In this very instant, the feint withdraws of itself: there is only truth there. But truth withdraws as well: it does not offer itself unclothed but as the *infinitely sharpened* point of the feint (and this point is its nudity, truth so bare that one sees its feint). At this extremity, which is always withdrawn yet always in excess over what might come to arrest it, the flash of being illuminates itself.

"Thought" only appears to be a predicate that comes and bestows quality upon this being. At the point of the cogito—at the extreme point of the feint—thought can only be identified by this structure of the feint, the structure of *extreme withdrawal*.

The structure of withdrawn fiction does not in fact belong to what we consider under the name "thought" (a term that Descartes specifies by *nothing* other, at the moment of the cogito, than the illumination of being that has just been described). The first model of this structure was provided by primitive *matter* in the fable of *The World*. Within the fiction, this matter was posited as "a chaos as confused and muddled as any the poets could invent" (AT XI 34/I.91). Yet:

> before I explain this at greater length, pause again for a bit to consider this chaos, and observe that it contains nothing which you do not know so perfectly that you could not even pretend to be ignorant of it. . . . And, as regards the matter from which I have composed it, there is nothing simpler or easier to know in inanimate creatures. The idea of this matter is included to such an extent in all the ideas that our imagination can form that you must necessarily conceive it or else you can never imagine anything at all. (AT XI 35/I.91–92)

The Fable of the invention of the World comprised its material cogito, or its *chaogito*. At the extreme, that is to say, at the initial point of fiction where the first gesture of creation fictions itself, fiction itself withdraws. If, as we have established, the fable's truth then lies in its invention, this truth is not only parallel or homologous to that of its content (the fictive creation): It functions only insofar as it invents within itself—or invents itself as—the veritable creation, the unfictionable origin of a world in general. True or feigned, an invented world remains the invention of a world. This is the point of the fable. Within this point, you cannot feign, you cannot be tricked [être feinté]. You are, and you cannot not be, just as the chaos, from which the world—or its fable—can arise, cannot not be conceived.

In the *Meditations*, the ultimate model of this structure will consist in the primordial position not of the "I think," but of the "I am, I exist." Between *The World* and the *Meditations*, the *Discourse* represents in this respect the weakest model in that the extremity of the withdrawal is immediately covered over, saturated, and guaranteed by the name of thought and by the formal mark of reasoning (*therefore*, I am).[25] But the "concept" of this name and its demonstrative "reason" reside in fact, as we now understand, in the conjunction of the other two models—in their impossible articulation:

Chaos—I am. *I am*—chaos.

On the other hand, the fabulous disposition of the *Discourse* operates the inoperable predication that we thus hear without understanding it. The fable recounts itself there as the fable of him who passes to the extremity of fiction, of *him who passes to the point of the fable's invention, where he withdraws.*

Such a point can only be the point where the fable is inaugurated, the point of fabulation itself, or of an invention of the fable such that no poetics is capable of describing it, and still less of prescribing it, and such that can only be summoned by the illumination of an autobiographical ontology.

That is, an ontology that blends with the invention of the discourse of my life, the invention of my life *as* discourse (or fable). The ontological locus, the place of substance is the place from where I utter this discourse. The invention blends with the utterance. It cannot take place in any place, in any antecedent or subjacent instance at the extremity of the feint, since this extremity bears the generalized fiction of the absence of every being and every truth. Thus, substance is here not sub-jacent; *it utters itself.* Or rather, it is the sub-jacency of the utterance to itself (and hence something completely different than the structural position of a "subject of the utterance")—the empty depth, the withdrawn cavity from which a voice is heard, that says, "I fabulate." In addition, we know that if the cogito teaches me *that* I am substance, it does not for all that teach me *what* this substance is. Except that it is "thinking," that is, "feigning."

The subject takes place insofar as he says *I feign*, insofar as he says *I fabulate*—or: *I am fabulating*—and insofar as he says this at such an extremity that he brings himself to the fable's origin, which also means that he transports the *fable* itself, withdrawn from fiction as well as truth, to the point where it illuminates its own etymology: *fari*, to speak, to say. *Cogito* does not say anything other than *for*.

For, I say, says he who invents the fable, who invents himself as the fable, or whom his fable invents. I discourse, says the Method. I emancipate myself from every affabulation as well as from every verification. I utter myself, I am. The Second Meditation will mark the mutual belonging of being and the moment of uttering: "this proposition, *I am, I exist*, is necessarily true whenever it is put forward by me or conceived in my mind" (AT VII 25/II.17). *Hoc pronuntiatum*: this proposition, in the sense of *this statement*. It is the statement itself that is true, which means that its truth consists only in its *utterance*, and not in the proposition's possible content or message. The statement here is of course not the same as the utterance, but the latter is the former's only content. (Hence we must also understand that the "it is conceived in my mind" is only a particular case of utterance—in the dialogue or monologue of the soul with itself.) I pronounce, I am. I pronounce *I*, I *am* pronouncing I.

This must be recognized, therefore, as the purest and most extreme form—that is, perhaps also as the extenuated form—of *performative* statement as it is conceived in linguistics. Benveniste's brief description will suffice here to characterize this kind of statement:

> The performative utterance [*énoncé*], being an act, has the property of being *unique*. It cannot be produced except in special circumstances, at one and only one time, at a definite date and place. It does not have the value of description or prescription but, once again, of performance. This is why it is often accompanied by indications of date, of place, of names of people, witnesses, etc.; in short, it is an event because it creates the event. Being an individual and historical act, a performative utterance cannot be repeated. Each reproduction is a new act performed by someone who is qualified.[26]

As a narrative, the *Discourse on the Method* as a whole then consists in accompanying the events, in telling "the story of my mind," which confers upon the *cogito*, or rather not upon *the* cogito but upon "cogito," this character of a unique event. However, unlike any other kind of event brought about by a performative (of the type "I declare the meeting open"), the event is here nothing other than the performation itself, or rather the *being* coextensive with this performation: *I am*. Such a being *is*—as certain and true being—only through and for the duration of its pronunciation. Hence *Cogito*, or from now on *for* (I say, I fabulate, I discourse, I perform, I am performing) is the performative of performation: the self-preformation, even the self-formation through the statement of the being of the one who utters as being of truth. The true being, *from now on identical to being-true*, does not consist in a statement any more than in the substance of someone who utters or in the position of an utterance (for substance, position, meaning of the statement are all performed in "cogito"). Rather, it consists in an *uttering*, in the *uttering* of the utterance, the one who utters, and the statement.[27]

To utter: *the uttering* [l'énoncer] consists in substantivizing the infinitive. This could also constitute, despite everything, and at least provisionally, a way of in-finitizing the substance, of stripping it of its completeness and its foundation, which is the only way of leaving out the already given subject of an utterance, since, at the extremity of the *cogito*, within "cogito," the subject has not yet taken place. Within the *uttering*, the subject loses all finish, all finition of figure: it is not, definitely not, infinite, yet it is not finite either. In-finite, it *is* not. And in the end, I must give up the desire to define it. The uttering includes this giving up. But I do not for all that give myself over to the ineffable of its birth as subject. Rather, I encounter within it the in-finite fable of the uttering.

In addition, if it is true, as pragmatic linguistics asserts, that all utterances are ultimately performatives,[28] the self-performation (where any self loses itself) of "cogito" is properly equivalent to "for," to a general or generalized "for," and the *cogito* rests upon the very possibility of language, while at the same time giving rise to this possibility. The Subject of metaphysics will have constituted itself, substantially, as *speaking subject*, as the subjected extremity of language, or more precisely of the proclamation. Hence, from now on, the logic of the extremity forbids that we ever grasp the event of this subject through any problematic of language: neither a linguistic essence of man, a law of the symbolic, nor a being-already-spoken will be able to either account for or overcome this *for*, internal and external to the speaking subject, internal and external to both the *subject* and *speech*. However, this *for* is neither a silence nor a noise. Both silence and noise are measured in relation to the already given articulation of a word. But at the extremity of *for*, it [*ça*] barely articulates *itself*. It opens itself: is it, again, a mimicking gesture? I will come back to it.

"I am" is *true* only when I say "I am." But "I am" says only "I am feigning," and "I am feigning" always ends up or begins (instantaneously) by meaning to say: *for*, I say. This does not mean anything, or means only the "meaning-to-say" itself.[29] The Fable-Discourse utters being—or knowledge—as the saying of a will for Saying. The autobiography that constitutes the text's narrative is the autobiography of this willing. The fable that makes a discourse out of it has this saying as its "instruction." The fable provides the lesson, the *lectio*, the recitation and repetition of: *I*—invent the saying.

The lesson is the pure *lectio*, and this is why the example of the Discourse is inimitable and its fable incredibly veridical. One cannot imitate the cogito, the *thought* of which is equivalent to the statement, or more exactly to the *uttering*. "It is put forward by me *or* conceived in my mind" establishes this equivalence, which the whole fable entailed and from which it proceeded, the equivalence of *cogito* and *for*. Statements may be imitated, but one does not imitate the act of uttering: the cogito cannot be said by an actor, it can only be said by Descartes, character of his own fable and actor of his own *for*.

Mundus est fabula: the world is the uttering, the *pure* subject is I who utters itself uttering. Pure and veritable fiction indeed, at the height of purity. As a result, the subject withdraws in it. Throughout centuries of subjectivity, there will never be any other I than the I withdrawn from its own discourse, and who will recite its fables, saying: "I am the State," or "Ego, Hugo," or "Madame Bovary, that is me," or again: "Great God! Why am I myself?"[30]

Everywhere in this world, the I withdraws within and from its *for*. And it is this *withdrawal*—which is, or rather makes neither absence nor rift, neither fiction nor truth, but forms the "subject" in a much more abysmally *intimate* way—it is this withdrawal that remains to be thought. That is to say, what remains to be thought is something that *is* not—neither a nature, nor a structure of the subject, not even it [*ça*]—but something that nevertheless makes up the very act of *ego*, its self-position in the form of: it withdraws *itself*, and this *happens* to it, at the extreme point of its fabulation—of its *saying*—like an accident through which the *self* becomes equivalent to *chaos*. As soon as I open the mouth, I withdraw. The place of this mouth does not let itself be circumscribed.

And what comes out of this mouth does not let itself be defined: Discourse on truth, life story, moral lesson are inextricably linked within it. Life of truth and truth of life form the chiasm of the Subject's ethics. Literature and philosophy have never meant anything else. But the lesson of the *Discourse* is the following: When this meaning-to-say utters itself in its absolute purity, at the extremity of willing (no matter what I want, I cannot doubt anymore) and of saying (it is still I who say that I cannot say anything true), this meaning-to-say exceeds its life as well as its truth. It withdraws of itself from itself [*se retranche de lui-même*]. A true Subject, a living Subject, in short, *a* Subject, never takes place. Nevertheless, something takes place in this nonplace, something like a speech that would tell you, for example: "You exist, and you know that you exist, and you know this because you know that you are doubting. But what are you—you who have doubts about everything but cannot doubt that you yourself exist?"[31]

Unum Quid

What must be in question here is a convulsion of Cartesian thought, and perhaps *its* convulsion. A convulsion is a complete wrenching away, a total tremor—the shaking of an edifice, which tightens, ties, and contracts its parts as much as it disjoints and disarticulates them, breaking the good order of the organization. It is a brutal and instantaneous disorder, which does not take the form of a dispersion or dismantlement but of an excessive tightening and interlocking. It is the spasm of a system, of muscles or concepts (but we will see that here it is a question of the system that joins together muscles and concepts), not when this system is subjected to an external cause of discord or corrosion but when it strikes against itself the violent blow of its own bond, of its contracture. And this does not happen without syncope: both words are not without analogy, combining a putting-together with a cutting or wrenching away, forcing the joint by tightening it rather than breaking it apart.

The question of the joint constitutes, in Descartes, the last question: that of the joining of the soul and the body. Its position and its difficulty are well known.[1] But not well known enough to have put an end to a discourse about the famous "Cartesian dualism," which some believe to be well established. There is no doubt that this "dualism" between the thinking and the extended substances occupies in Descartes all the room that is usually attributed to it. But there is also no doubt either (at least, this is what we will try to prove in what follows) that the rigorous partitioning [*partage*] between both substances happens wholly in keeping with an aim and exigency, the ultimate end of which is the *union* of the soul and the body. As such, all that modernity has never stopped investing up until now in the reconstruction of a "psychophysical," "psychophysiological," or "psychosomatic" unity of the human being (nothing less, then, than the entire field of the so-called human sciences, of culture, milieu, or discourse, including the outcomes or substitutes of these disappointing sciences: from saunas to yoga, from theaters to treatises, the whole panting celebration of bodies, with or without organs, but always places of a soul that does not dare say its name)—all this constant anti-Cartesian demand for a *re-incarnation* proceeds directly from Descartes and repeats his ultimate gesture, but perhaps without being able to recognize its convulsive constraint.

It is indeed with Descartes that the Incarnation ceases to offer itself as the revelation of a mystery and becomes the obfuscation of its own desire.

As we all know, the union of the soul and the body is established in the Sixth Meditation: "Nature also teaches me, by these sensations of pain, hunger, thirst and so on, that I am not merely present in my body as a sailor is present in a ship, but that I am very closely joined and, as it were, intermingled with it, so that I and the body form a unit [*me non tantum adesse meo corpori ut nauta adest navigio, sed illi arctissime esse conjunctum et quasi permixtum, adeo ut unum quid cum illo componam*]" (AT VII 81/II.56). Because the phrase *unum quid* cannot be translated into French literally, the Duc de Luynes was forced to displace slightly the accent in the description of the union: the hesitation and the limitation introduced by the *quasi* has been transferred from the *permixtio* to the "unit."[2] The Latin text says: I am almost mixed with my body to the point that I compose with it a certain unity, a something that is one: *unum quid*. The displacement of the *quasi* does not touch on anything important, and the Latin *unum quid* is nonetheless thought even if not grammatically constructed in relation to the *quasi*. Yet, Descartes wrote this *unum quid*, and we shall have to keep our eyes fixed on it, so to speak.[3]

What about this unity of the soul and the body, what about this thing whose unity certainly does not precede the *compositio* that produced it, but whose being-one is given by opposition to the simple being-together or being-alongside—the *adesse* of the sailor—and hence according to the effect of a conjunction that implies a union, that is, in a certain way, a mixing, interpenetration, and reciprocity between the two components—*unio et quasi permixtio mentis cum corpore* [the union and, as it were, intermingling of the mind with the body], as the text says a couple of lines below? What about the *unum quid* whose *unum* seems well supported, but whose *quid* remains suspended upon its own unity as well as upon the interval of the *quasi*?

It is not necessary to go back over Gueroult's analysis of the "sensations" that make possible "nature"'s teaching of this union: pain, hunger, thirst, and so on indicate the finality rather than the truth of this knowledge. Hence, the guarantee of such knowledge implies a specific way divine truthfulness functions. Here, it is by virtue of His goodness, and of the principle of the best that derives from it, that God guarantees the truth, not of the reality of things (as this *quid*) but of the teleological function of their assemblage.

The correctness of this analysis is not in question, and it is not my intention to propose another critical analysis of the reasons supporting the authentication, in the system of the reality of the two substances, of the functional truth of their union. At most it would have to be pointed out, if one wanted to go down such a path, that the *position* of this truth as a truth about a function and a finality cannot on its own completely account for the *nature* of this truth, that is, precisely the substantial union as such. Of course, this is what is implied by Gueroult's argument when he distinguishes between the veracity that guarantees this function and the one that guarantees a reality in general. But the fact remains that Descartes speaks expressly in favor of the *reality* of this union (which is perfectly compatible with the claim that there is "no reality in the composite substance other than the reality of its constituents").[4] Are we not forced, as a result, to underscore the fact that the finality that justifies the union functionally did not necessitate, in the final analysis, the affirmation of the reality of this union? This is what Gueroult himself implicitly recognizes when he recalls in passing, and without dwelling on it, that the same teleological function will be found in Malebranche but coupled with a *refusal* of substantial union.[5] The demonstration through finality, as irrefutable as it is, would leave out of reach the *necessity* of the support chosen by Descartes to be the bearer of this function. Hence, we do not ask: How is the union of the soul and the body justified? Instead, we ask: Why is such a union *needed* (where, for example, a divine calculation would have sufficed)? According to what necessity must the *function* (that of providing me with information about the external world insofar as my preservation is interested in it) be, as such, determined in terms of *being* or reality? Why must the substantial union be real?

Perhaps it would be useful to start from what is well known, but which an irresistible inclination of the tradition leads us to misunderstand again and again. It is also in the Sixth Meditation, and only there, that it is established that the body does not think.[6] Consequently, the establishment of the *cogito* in the Second Meditation does not rest upon the separation between the soul and the body. We should also recall here that this all-too-famous *cogito* first takes, as a matter of principle, the form of the statement: "*I am, I exist.*" Contrary to what certain interpreters have maintained, "*ego sum, ego existo*" nowhere entails any "existentiality," in the modern sense of the term, of the *cogito*, any more than an existentialism on Descartes's part.[7] Here, the *existo* is determined by the *ego*—by the first person of the utterance—and not the other way around. But even so, the *ego* does not entail its existence as substance distinct from the body. If it is certain, as the same Meditation is quick to assert, that "I am not that structure [*compages*] of limbs which is called a human body" (AT VII 27/II.18) (a formula that lets us believe, in fact, that this "structure" as a mere assemblage might not be, strictly speaking, the *human* body), it is because it is certain that I am not my body insofar as I utter *ego*, that is, insofar as I think *in the sense* in which all thought entails (or is defined by) this uttering self-position of the *ego*. Which does not rule out that in determining that "I am only a thing that thinks," I still only determine a *part* of me, as the Third Meditation will say, "since I am now concerned only and precisely with that part of me which is a thinking thing" (AT VII 49/II.34). The *I* that posits itself in the uttering of *ego sum* does not exhaust the nature or the substance of me [*du moi*], or at least such nature is not exhausted by "pure thought."[8] The proof is that this same "thing that thinks" is also the one who "is willing," "desires," "imagines," and "has sensory perceptions" (AT VII 28/II.19), operations that will all be confirmed in their corporeal determination. In other words, at the stage of the Second Meditation—a stage that lasts in this regard until the sixth—I do not know whether I have a body, or whether it is possible that I only believe that I have one: "Yet I certainly seem to see [*et certe videre videor*] . . . what is called 'having a sensory perception' is strictly just this" (AT VII 29/II.19). This proves that this most proper *sensing*—evidence itself, by opposition to every syllogism[9]—which rests wholly upon and consists only in the feint, implies nothing other than the fiction that allows it to be established. Hence, it implies nothing specifically with regard to the real nature of the subject of this sensing, and hence does not entail its "spirituality" any more than its "corporeality." Having been taken to task by the second set of Objections about this regime of the "fiction of the mind" in which the Second Meditation unfolds, Descartes recalls the latter's text: "Yet may it not perhaps be the case that these very things which I am supposing to be nothing, because they are unknown to me, are in reality identical with the 'I' of which I am aware? I do not know, and for the moment I shall not argue the point." And he adds: "Here I wanted to give the reader an express warning that at that stage I was not yet asking whether the mind is distinct from the body" (AT VII 129/II.93).

   Must we insist? The fundamental movement of the *Meditations* is not that of a detour *through* a fiction from which we ought then to return (as from some demonstrative device) to reality. It is that of a feint *as* the self-position of the I, a feint that provides at the same time the endpoint and the source of every real demonstration. If it was a question of passing *through* a fiction, we would indeed be supposing for a time that I do not have a body. But in fact what is established is that I attest my existence all the more certainly if I feign *not only* to lack a body *but also*, and just as much, to lack thought. What is established in this way is that I cannot feign that I am not feigning: whereby, in effect, nothing has been said about the nature of the *I* that feigns, and it has not been said "whether the mind is distinct from the body."[10] The feint has related to itself—and only to itself—as the indubitable being of the feigning subject, but the *being-feint* of the subject does not imply in any way the "being-feigned" (the fictitiousness or the fictionality) of the nature of this being, and more specifically of its potential corporeal nature. The feint-structure of the most proper "sensing" has nothing to do with the fictive nature of a sensing subject, intellectual or corporeal, or intellectual and corporeal. This does not mean, however, that this feint-structure—this being-feint that *is* nothing else than this structure—necessarily entails a real union of the soul and the body. More simply, but also more decisively, it does not entail anything with regard to the substance, neither duality nor union, because it has nothing directly to do with the position or the qualification of the substance.

The distinction between substances is put to work in the Sixth Meditation.[11] In other words, it is at the moment where the reality of the world needs to be proven that it becomes necessary to secure the independence of the thinking reality. It is not necessary here to demonstrate once again the mechanism of this proof. Let us rather focus on what the proof of the distinction actually proves, so that we can understand to which necessity this operation responds, and the relation this necessity entertains with the necessity of the proof of the union, which can seem to contradict the former or at least to remain heterogeneous to it.

The real distinction between the soul and the body is thus proven. Or again, it is proven that the *ego* that thinks is not, as such, a body. However, this result is not given in such a simple way under this simple or too simple form, and which would still need to be interpreted so that we can understand what it means. At least three determinations inevitably follow from the result, imparting it with its exact scope:[12]

1. If the proof implies that the things I conceive as distinct are in fact so (and divine truthfulness assures me of it), it is because these things "are capable of being separated [*être posées séparément*]" (AT VII 78/II.54). However, in the case under consideration of the soul and the body, nothing assures me that this *possibility* is ever actualized in one way or another, nor that I am capable of apprehending its effectivity. This is why the text of the Meditation[13] specifies that these things "are capable of being separated, at least by God." Hence, if the conception of the cogito was fully equivalent to its position in being (or as being), the conception of the distinction, for its part, is equivalent to such a position only from the point of view of God. *For me*, however, the proof of the distinction involves a certain actual indistinction. In other words, the certainty of the autonomy of the thinking thing does not lead to the independent existence of something like a "pure mind."[14] It follows that there might not be—at least not for me, even though there might for God—any other appre-hension of the existence of thought than the one that takes place in and as the apprehension of my existence—*ego existo*—in which the *ego* is not determined as independent substance, but—and this is quite different—as thinking existence.[15]

2. Insofar as the proof concludes that the thinking substance is really distinct, it does not for all that produce any positive knowledge of the nature of this substance: "When I added that the mind is not extended, I did not intend to explain what the mind is, but merely to point out that those who think it is extended are in error" (AT VII 388/II.266). This does not mean that we do not know the mind. The same text reminded us of it a bit earlier: "our knowledge of a thinking thing is much more extensive than . . . our knowledge of anything else" (AT VII 387/II.266). But this extensiveness is not necessarily a completeness. The same text shows it too, since when Gassendi objects that he does not know this thing that thinks any better than a blind person knows the sun when he conceives of it as a "heating thing," Descartes replies: "the only people who can prove that the idea of the sun formed by the blind man does not contain everything that can be perceived of the sun are those who are endowed with sight and detect in addition its light and shape" (ibid.). It is clear that if Descartes knows about the thinking thing everything that a human being can know of it, it is still possible that human beings do not know more about it than the blind person about the sun. Human beings, perhaps, know only of the "heat" of this substance, and nothing of its "figure" or "light" (*lux* rather than *lumen*, therefore). Hence, the knowledge of the distinction does

not lead to absolute certainty with regard to the immortality of the mind, and neither does it exclude that I do not or not yet know other properties that belong to the distinct substances as such, for example, the property of their union . . .

3. The real distinction[16] that is thus proven is the distinction of this I, "that is, my soul, by which I am what I am."[17] With regard to "me," we see that the "thing" that is distinguished in this way represents at the same time—and oddly—the whole and the part. At the same time, *I* am distinct from my body (insofar as I am a thing that thinks), and this *me* is only me insofar as it constitutes that by which "I am what I am," which does not exclude that *I* perhaps be something more than that *by which* I am *what* I am. Which does not exclude that *I* be still something more than that by which I am *this*, that I am [*je suis* ça, *que je suis*]. It is undoubtedly for this reason that right when he derives the distinction between the substances, Descartes already points out in advance the union that will be proven later: "It is true that I may have (or, to anticipate, that I certainly have) a body that is very closely joined to me. But nevertheless . . . it is certain that I, etc." (AT VII 78/II.54).

What Descartes keeps open is the possibility (the future certainty of which he announces) that I contain the property of a very close conjunction—*valde arcte conjunctum*—with what I am not. And hence that I may still be something more than what I am essentially, without, as the rest of the Meditation will show, this conjunction being posited as a mere accident in relation to this essence. The union that is anticipated in the distinction—and is anticipated as its apparent contradiction (It is true that I may . . . But nevertheless . . .)—will neither be added to the thinking substance as an external accident, nor will it inversely modify the "essence" or "nature" of this substance. In the gap between these two possibilities, the proof of the distinction opens the space for what could be called a singularly double status of "me"—of a strange couple of forces, disjunction and contraction at the same time, exerting themselves on me.

Perhaps it is not impossible to begin to give an account of this *singular duality*, and all the traits that we have just emphasized, starting from the very text upon which we have just relied. Indeed, the French translation includes a significant addition in comparison to the first Latin version. The latter said: "*certum est a corpore meo revera esse distinctum,*" and not "*moi, c'est-à-dire mon âme, par laquelle je suis ce que je suis* [me, that is my soul, by which I am what I am]." Clearly, the Duc de Luynes did not take the sole responsibility or, most likely, the initiative for such an addition, and it must be attributed to Descartes.

To what concern does such an addition correspond if not that of trying to avoid writing what the French language made more conspicuous than the Latin, namely: "it is certain that *I* am really distinct from *my* body"[18] (since the Latin sentence did not here take the form *ego sum distinctus*)? In writing this sentence, it was to the totality of the *I* that the distinction applied, without any precision or restriction, and of the *I* in the subject position (of the active subject, if we can say so in order to oppose it to the Latin *me*, which is the subject of an infinitive clause). What *I am*—the whole and veritable being of what *I am* that affirmed itself as existing in the statement of this existence, and without having to examine whether "the mind is distinct from the body"—must be distinguished from that *by which* I am what I am. And it is in the same movement that "I, that is, *my soul*" distinguishes itself from *my body*. Consequently, the distinction is well formed only if it is posited *simultaneously* between me and the body *and* between two things that are *mine*—two things that belong to me, and perhaps two things that are me, or in the in-between-two-things of me.

This distinction cannot be reduced to that between *being* and *having*. Of course, I *am* a thinking thing, while I *have* a body. But I *am* united to this body. The closeness of the union, its tightening (*valde arcte*), its *permixtio*, means precisely that it cannot be reduced to an extrinsic relation of having. Unless Descartes introduces here the general question of the *being of having*, of the being of property as possession, a question that perhaps remains to be extracted from a whole tradition (philosophical, political, economic) for which being as property (and also under the form of "one's own body" or the "body proper") is opposed to the impropriety of having . . .

However that may be, my *soul*, here, certainly represents this *me* by which (but what does this *by* mean? what relation of part, means, principle, agent, determinant, could be invoked to fill in this *by*?) I am *this* that I am [*je suis ça que je suis*]. But *my* soul certainly does not represent—at least not in a simple way, not in a *clear-cut* way—this *me* who should be the subject of the proposition (it is certain that I am) and who, by a strange syllepsis (it is certain that I . . . is entirely distinct)[19] and while remaining the lawful subject, in fact gives up its place to the third person—a feminine third person no less—of the soul. The syllepsis—by joining what should not be joined—highlights the nonconsecution from the *I*-thinking-substance[20] to the *I*-subject of the uttering existence. It inscribes in the *same* the nonconsecution from the substance to the subject, which might make up the ground of this modern inauguration of the Subject.

When I utter: me . . . is substance, I give the position of the substance. But the pre-supposition of this position (presupposition in which the very substantiality of the substance resides) consists in the first-person statement that alone makes the position possible: I am me who is substance. In this statement, and *from* this statement, the subject identifies itself with the (thinking) substance and distinguishes itself from it *at the same time*. The proof of the distinction between the soul and the body involves at once a conclusion: the subject-substance that thinks is wholly distinct from extension and, according to the logic of a syllepsis, an implication (which consists only in the persistence of the inaugural cogito): the subject is also *distinct from the distinction* between the two substances.

There is thus the distinction between substances, and the distinction between the subject and the distinction between substances.

No matter how strange it might seem, these two distinctions are nonetheless, in a certain way, the same. It is always a question of the distinction between the substance-subject and the extended substance. But it is precisely to the extent that we discern their identity that we also recognize the necessity of distinguishing them.

Their identity consists in the predominantly negative scope of the distinction between the soul and the body. This distinction posits that the soul *is not* of the order of the body, is not extended. The *ego* of the *cogito*, in a similar way, distinguishes itself negatively: It *is not* of the order in which it is necessary to distinguish between substances. The articulation of these two negations must be analyzed.

In establishing the soul independently of the body, Descartes, as we have seen, mostly wants to "point out that those who think it is extended are in error." The same text, a couple of lines further, specifies the scope and reason for this warning: "Even though the mind is united to the whole body, it does not follow that it is extended throughout the body, since it is not in its nature to be extended, but only to think" (AT VII 388–389/II.266).

Once more, the affirmation of the distinction is accompanied by the anticipation of the union and of the kind of restriction it includes. But this time, the restriction is used to determine precisely the object of the distinction: the mind *is* not extended, in itself, properly and as such. Which does not prevent it from being in a relation of union with extension—with this extension that is the body—and in a relation without reserve: The mind is united with the *whole* body. Yet, if we read the preceding text attentively again, this totality of the union prevents us from understanding as a restriction what grammatically looks like one (*even though* . . .). Descartes does not set aside or restrict the union as a kind of enclave or exception— dare we say as a sort of foreign body?—in the midst of the regime of the distinction. For the union would then be thought as a *part*—set aside—of both substances. In this case, the inconvenience would not consist, first and foremost, in the fact we would be affirming that the mind is extended at least in this part—be it only a point[21]—but rather that it would limit the union. The union, however, must be total—we will get to understand this totality better in a moment. And it is for this reason that the distinction must be absolute: Rather than disperse itself *throughout* the body, *only that which is not extended can* unify itself *to* the body.

The nonextension of the mind appears, therefore, both as that which the union requires and as that which the distinction guarantees. What is both required and guaranteed in this way is the unity of the subject as his own truth.

If the mind were extended—partes extra partes—it would not only be divisible, but always already divided. It would not be the unity of *ego*. The distinction between the soul and the body guarantees this unity, which in turn is required so that a total union be possible (and not a mere interlocking of parts), the logic of which can only be that of the distinction between the ego *and* the distinction between substances.

This does not mean that the ego has previously been constituted as an independent and available thing, structured according to a unity, or if one wants, as a reality with a unitary nature symmetrically opposed to plural extension. It does not mean that the ego has been predetermined as the unitary content of truth. It means, rather, that because "truth is essentially indivisible" (AT VII 548/II.374), it is through the exclusion (in doubt) of *all* truth-contents and of *all* real positions that the truth has been produced as utterance: *ego* (sum). As such (but what is the utterance *as such*? what is *that*? thing, reality, act, moment, event, structure? what *is* the *uttering*?), the truth has not been produced as a substance that would have been brought to light and made known. It is rather substantiality that has been produced *only* as self-uttering "punctuality": *ego* (since, as we see very well, and even if we do not *see* it, at least it *lets itself be heard*, we cannot even speak of a self-uttering *of the* ego). This is why the Second Meditation did not yet take a stand on the issue of the substantial nature of the ego.

Consequently, when Descartes comes to posit the mind as a distinct substance, he actually carries out a double operation:

1. He *substantivizes* the "pure" uttering: *ego* (if it is possible to point to such a thing as a "pure" utterance); that is, he properly installs the *ego* in the position of the *sub-jectum* as Heidegger analyzed it, the position of what is "constant and standing [*das Ständige und das Stehende*]"[22] as permanent subject of representation, and hence as "the represemter itself [*das Vorstellende selbst*]"[23] who makes up the sub-strate of the modern regime of truth as certainty. To this extent, Descartes notes that the utterance: *ego* has always-already pre-supposed itself as position of a sub-strate, hence pre-supposing "that *subiectum* and *ego*, that subjectivity and egoity [*Ichheit*] become equivalent."[24]

2. But what Descartes distinguishes here in establishing it as sub-stance is at the same time nothing else or nothing more than *distinction itself*, that is, this absolute distinction that can only appear with "*ego*": saying *I* is not to say any*thing* distinct, or to posit a distinct substance, but to produce the distinction from every thing (and from every *judgment* with regard to the reality and/ or the truth of a thing). I withdraw, and I distinguish myself: It is *I* who distinguishes and withdraws *me*.

In Descartes's discourse, the first of these operations is superimposed upon and hides the second. This is so because the second is not supported

by a discourse, but only by . . . saying: *I*—consequently it needs the first operation in order to support itself beyond this saying. But this operation of
support—this sub-stantial operation—is only there in accordance with an
unsustainable saying: I (unsustainable in its absolute distinction).

Not conceiving the distinction of the mind would therefore mean not
conceiving *the* distinction: *ego* (who, as we said, is undoubtedly inconceiv-
able as such), and being condemned never to conceive anything. For not conceiving *the* distinction—ego—would mean not conceiving the self-position
of conception itself in the utterance of *ego*, which is responsible for the fact
that I think, since "by the term 'thought,' I understand everything which
we are aware of as happening within us, in so far as we have awareness of
it,"[25] and I also understand that this immediate awareness is not reflexive,
does not have any way of grasping *itself* in a specular way, as Descartes has
repeatedly pointed out.[26]

Originally, therefore, the distinction is "consubstantial" with the *cogito*,
in a sense that we could call presubstantial, prior and external to the position of substances and their reciprocal distinction. The distinction between
the soul and the body is secondary and derived in relation to *ego who distinguishes itself*, and it is only made in order to secure or support the originary
distinction. And it does this by guaranteeing that *ego* has the nature of a *thing*
that thinks. For *ego*, who "stands," so to speak, only on the outermost tip of
its utterance—ego, who is no other "thing" than the withdrawal within and
from its own *for*.[27] As soon as it is understood as a thing that thinks, *the* ego
is satisfied with this designation of "thing," even though it does not entail a
veritable determination of the nature of this thing. In truth, knowledge
of the nature of the thinking thing is so little or so badly secured that
Descartes could write:

> It is also false, *or at least asserted without the slightest supporting reason*, that some
> thinking substance is divisible. . . . In fact we cannot understand thought to
> possess any extension or divisibility, and it is wholly absurd to put this forward
> as a true claim *when it has neither been revealed by God nor established by our
> intellect*. (AT VII 520/II.354; emphasis added, J.-L. N.)[28]

If the divisibility of the thinking substance is not purely and simply false, it
is because its indivisibility is not absolutely *proven*: it is only necessary with

regard to our capacity of conception. Such a hesitation can only be understood insofar as Descartes is here speaking about a thinking *substance*; the hesitation would not, and indeed did not, have any reason to occur with regard to the *cogito*, with regard to *ego* who thinks. For the immediacy of the latter confers upon it *ispo facto* an indivisible simplicity, but this simplicity is precisely not conferred upon it as substance.

The substantial distinction between the soul and the body aims to secure the indivisibility of *ego*, which has never been secured except by means of the constitutive precariousness and instability of its "pure" self-utterance, by bestowing upon it the nature of a thing or reality (but without being able to produce absolute certainty about it, as we have just read). In that case one should dare to say that the distinction between the soul and the body plays a functional—or supporting—role in the Cartesian theory, whereas the ontology to which it refers would be the ontology of *ego* insofar as it distinguishes *itself* while uttering itself, and hence insofar as it "posits" itself as distinct from the distinction between substances.

Both distinctions—and their reciprocal distinction—make up a system in which the *union*, far from being added uneasily as an excess, is, so to speak, self-evident.

On the one hand, the distinction between substances, provided it is posited in the right way, gives itself as the distinction between two things that are absolutely incommensurable. By virtue of the first distinction, which remains in the background, they are incommensurable to the point that one of these two substances, the extended thing, could be said to be the only one to have the authentic figure of substance: foundation [*assise*], substrate, support for any thing that can be posited and can occupy a place (any place), while the other, the thinking thing, supports itself only through the immediate and instantaneous grasp of a substantiality that consists in nothing else than this immediacy and instantaneity, and that, consequently, *does not take place*. Now, it is exactly because of this total incommensurability that the union is possible; the question is not how two heterogeneous supports can be joined together, since it is not a question of a joining-together (concept related to extension) but of the union between two things *so different from one another that one cannot be an obstacle for the other.*[29] An extended mind might have some trouble in occupying an extended body; moreover, it could only *occupy* the body, be it in part or as a whole (yet "I am not merely present in my body as a sailor is present in a ship"). The nonextension of the mind can, on the contrary, be "united to the whole body"—*quasi permixtum.*

On the other hand, the distinction of *ego*, insofar as it is the distinction of what has, so to speak, no really substantial substantiality—but it is not a *what*, it is the *what* that is only I, that consists only in the *I* (who say I). This distinction, which is only the *distingo* of the *for*, raises (or, more precisely, does not raise) the question of the existential status that *I* bestows upon itself, that *I* as such (or the *for* as such) consists in bestowing upon itself. Therefore, it raises (or does not raise) the question of a nonsubstantial *status*, of a constitutive *instability.*[30] In short, instability of the *sum* that grasps itself in the *for*. Yet, the status of this insubstantial substance is precisely identical to its apprehension: *ego sum* is true "whenever *I* pronounce it or whenever *I* conceive it in my mind" (it is *I* who underline *I*).[31] This "status"—that of evidence—necessarily has the structure of immediacy as *self*-relation. To this extent, it is equivalent—with regard to its structure—to the immediate apprehension of the union of the soul and the body, as we will examine it in a moment.

Should we say, on the contrary, that the apprehension of the union is different in nature than that of the *ego* because the latter is intellectual while the former seems to be sensible: "what belongs to the union of the soul and the body . . . is known very clearly by the senses"[32]? We easily understand, however, that Descartes in this sentence underlines the *very clearly* of this *knowledge* as much as, if not more than, the senses that happen to provide this clarity. Besides, Descartes will write in the *Principles of Philosophy* that our "soul" knows the union "by means of a natural knowledge."[33] The proof of the union does not substitute a coarsely immediate sensuous or existential certainty for intellectual clarity. Rather, it transposes certainty and clarity to the level of the senses, but this transposition is barely one since everything is played out at the same extreme point of immediate evidence. Thus, the distinction of the *ego*—which is independent from the distinction between the substances and precedes it—does not forbid the evidence of the union, but it does not establish it either (but is it a question of *establishing* anything?). More simply and more radically, both are played out in the *same* point.

Of course, this eliminates neither the difficulty nor the obscurity of the "proof" of the union, nor the awkwardness of Descartes's texts where this union is invoked.[34] What happens at this double and identical point, twice distinct from the distinction between substances—point of *ego* and point of union, point of *unum quid*—is that the evidential structure is introduced for the second time in this *same* that we believed to be of a purely intellectual nature, and is reintroduced as sensuous opacity (since it is the opacity of the senses—for the intellect—that provides us with clarity here . . .). How can evidence redouble itself into opacity in this way, and why must it do so, if not because what we believed was apprehending itself as intellectual evidence (without yet being guaranteed as distinct substance), and precisely because this evidence takes place without any shred of reflection, only consists in the obscurity that *constitutes* the instantaneity of clarity? Let us stay with the photographic metaphor for a while. If *ego* sees itself in the snapshot [*l'instantané*] that allows the luminous trace of its unstable image to be inscribed (but is it an image? it is an utterance, an uttering, at most the opening of a mouth . . .), this vision and this inscription themselves depend on—in truth they do more than depend on it, they are "consubstantial" with—the instantaneous closing (the instant "is" also instability) of the diaphragm through which light passes. The evidence of the *cogito* has the nature of a *diaphragm*. It is what gets in the way of something, obstructing or blocking it.

In the brutal closing of the diaphragm of its certainty, the Subject convulses. A contracture more powerful than mere evidence—but which is the mechanism of this evidence—fixes it in the pose of Subject and hence unites it with itself, but this pose disarticulates it, or contracts its articulation up to the point of deformity. The distinction of ego—the gaping of a mouth contracted on *ego*—is not clear and distinct; or rather: This distinction does not distinguish itself from the opaque evidence of the union.

The evidence of ego's being comes to the subject through a very different path than that of a recognition, reflection, or speculation. It is not a matter of a "mirror stage," but of something prior to any "stage," "station," or "stasis" of the subject.[35] *Ego* posits itself, imposes itself, happens and comes to itself less through the gathering into an image of its *membra disjecta* than through the convulsion in which it tears itself apart and binds itself together at the same time, in a punctual identity that would itself be prior to this convulsion if it were ever able to take place. But such an identity, the unique uniqueness of the pure point of Subject, only occurs at its own extremity, in a spasm that articulates and dismembers it, that articulates it only in dismembering it.

This is in fact why the substance that is distinguished after the fact as the essence of the ego can be said to be incomplete in a sense. An incomplete substance is a contradiction, Descartes knows that well and says it.[36] But he nevertheless adds: "It is also possible to call a substance incomplete in the sense that, although it has nothing incomplete about it *qua* substance, it is incomplete in so far as it is referred to some other substance in conjunction with which it forms something which is a unity in its own right" (AT VII 222/II.157). Would the necessity of the union lead to such an odd formulation—"substances incomplete *in a sense*"—if the union happened clearly from the outside as a mere accident to each substance? Would it not suffice to say that the substances are complete, and that the completeness can, *moreover*, be united? If Descartes does not say that, it is because the union can under no circumstances be understood as an external joining-together, as an interlocking, and this for the same reason that we already know. An interlocking—that of the sailor in his ship—could not prevent the thinking substance to be subjected in one way or another to the exigencies of extension. It is really the *cogito* that leads to the incompleteness of the thinking substance: The *cogito* must have absolutely nothing in common with the *partes extra partes*, and hence it requires a union that, in its own proper mode of union, has nothing to do with an assemblage of parts. *That* must be like *ego* in the mouth.

Thus, from the moment that thought thinks itself as the pure self-presence of the proclamation of *ego*—where thought thinks itself in principle as pure self-utterance, as pure self-uttering, excluding all thought-content and all discursivity—the substantiality of this substance *must* prove to be incomplete. It indeed proves to be so, despite Descartes's distinction (a distinction that, this time, is at play *within* the substance itself . . . and distinguishes itself again from the distinction *between* substances) between the substance "*qua* substance" and the substance "in so far as it is referred to some other substance." For the whole proposition means that this *relation* belongs essentially to the substantiality of the substance—or that the substance *qua* substance is as well the substance *qua* relation to another (at least in the case of the soul and the body, the only case where such an issue arises regarding the substance).[37] This circumstance is aggravated again by the fact that the relation produces a "unity in its own right [*un tout par soi*]": What is a "unity in its own right" if not a substance? Descartes never said that the *human being* was a substance, but he calls it again and again a "unity in its own right" or something that exists "from itself," an *ens per se*. What does this mean if not that it is a substance that cannot, does not want, or dare not say its name?

Now, what is substantiality? In the tradition that Descartes makes use of and diverts, it is the fact of being a subject, a *subjectum*, rather than of belonging to a subject. The human being is hence a subject that cannot be named or posited as such. It is the subject that cannot be sub-jected.

This is the fundamental reason[38] why the union is at the same time necessary and difficult, not to say impossible, to *establish*. In being thought for the first time *as* the structure of the sub-jectum *itself*, thought undergoes here a double ordeal. First, it cannot only be the thought of the *human being*, of the only self-identity available as self-exponible, simply because the one who thinks has not yet thought himself, even though he already has thoughts, either as God, or as animal. And second, the thought of the human being *as subject* withdraws in the instant of its exposition. It withdraws in the union as well as in the *for*.

But it is also because the union is the status of the *for*: I pronounce or I conceive, I move my tongue or I cogitate, I open my mouth or my mind, I speak *and* I think, I speak while thinking, I think while speaking. The *human being* is the subject of speaking thought, not in the sense of discourse but of the uttering. And this subject, as soon as he appears, already exhibits as his ownmost structure the incompleteness of his substance. The human subject has never been a figure that appeared and then disappeared within history,[39] for the unique reason that he has never conquered his figure of subject. His thinking will only have been his convulsion, the violent contraction of the instability of the substance upon the very substance of dispersion: *unum quid*, improbable unity of thought and extension.

Hence the strange and improbable paths of the proof. The analysis of this proof of the union as a proof by means of ends and by means of functions does not satisfy the requirements of the *ontological* status of the union, which Descartes calls *substantial* (union of the substances, but also *as* substance, even though it does not make up a third substance).[40] Such an analysis is legitimate, no doubt, and it indicates what will hitherto constitute the regime of the human being: the nexus of functions and ends in which the human being continues to strangle himself again and again. But at the same time as it opened the way for the functional human being, and as if through the reverse side of the same gesture, Descartes initiated the exorbitant existence of a subject who was not, could not, and ought not to either be substance or function.

In this interpretation, the path of the *cogito* does not let itself be distinguished at all, or at least not well, from that of the *union*. For both, it is a matter of an *experience* the concept of which evades in advance all epistemological as well as existential attempts at determination.

"The fact that the mind is closely conjoined with the body," the Replies to Arnaud say, "we experience constantly" (AT VII 227–228/II.160). It also forms the substance of Descartes's famous letter to Elizabeth from 1643 where all the traits of the certainty of the union are collected. It is experience. What is an experience? Is it not the very model of certainty?

> I would never have believed that there has ever existed anyone so dull that
> he had to be told what existence is before being able to conclude and assert that
> he exists. The same applies to doubt and thought. Furthermore, the only way
> we can learn such things is by ourselves: what convinces us of them is simply
> our own experience or awareness. (AT X 524/II.417–418)[41]

Our own experience: it is a matter of the experience *of ownness* [du propre], and there is no other kind of experience for Descartes. And the experience of ownness, for the soul, is as much that of its pure distinction from the body than that of a certain corporeality: "if we count as corporeal whatever belongs to a body, even though not of the same nature as body, then even the mind can be called corporeal, in so far as it is made to be unity to the body."[42]

The experience of ownness is ownness as experience; the soul is properly that which, in uttering itself, feels itself [*s'éprouve*] existing (an ordeal [*épreuve*] prior to any passion or affect, but that constitutes a proof [*fait preuve*]) and which, feeling itself existing in this way, experiences itself as properly united to the body. Even though it is never said explicitly, the experience of the union must be implied—be it only obscurely—in that of the cogito. What I experience constantly, how would I not experience it also, and perhaps first and foremost, each time I say: I am, I exist. It is *unum quid* who pronounces *ego*. And it is this experience, single and double at the same time, that remains, at the moment where it takes place, impossible to *establish*. "Constantly," "each time," it is what happens immediately without being produced, constructed, or demonstrated. *Unum quid*, a something that is neither-soul-nor-body, opens its mouth and pronounces or conceives: *ego sum*. Besides, this is still saying too much. *Unum quid* does not *have* a mouth that it could manipulate and open, no more than it has an intellect that it could exert to reflect upon itself. But something—*unum quid*—opens (it would therefore have the appearance or shape of a mouth) and this opening articulates itself (it would therefore have the appearance of discourse, hence of thought), and this articulated opening, in an extreme contraction, forms: *I*.

As a result, convulsed, it forms *itself* into an *I*, it feels itself *I*, it thinks itself *I*. *I* touches and fixes itself making—saying—*I*. Imagine a faceless mouth (that is, once again, the structure of the *mask*: the opening of the holes, and the mouth opening in the middle of the eye; the place of vision and theory diaphragmatically traversed, opened and closed at the same time, by a proclamation)—a faceless mouth, then, forming the ring of its contracture around the noise: *I*. "You" undergo this experience constantly, each time you put forward or conceive in your mind *ego*, each time—it happens to you constantly—you form the *o* of the first person (*first*, before it there is nothing): eg*o* cogit*o* exist*o*. An *O* forms the immediate loop of your experience. Truly, it is the experience of *that*—and it *makes* or *forms* it because it cannot *be* it.

The experience of the subject has nothing to do with the order of the empirical, nor with that of an existential intimacy. It builds the structure of the substance when the latter becomes the modern Subject. In this experience, the Subject apprehends his own *sub-stare* to the extent in which he does not grasp it as the *object* of an action or a thought (whether discursive or intuitive, for intuition is a concept that is present in the *Regulae* but not in the *Meditations*, which exceed all thought). The evidence of the *cogito* stands underneath every faculty and every substantiality. Cartesian experience is the experience of the *sub* without stasis or stance. Up to the end and without reserve—*ex-perior*—the *sub* puts to the test what it can be. *Ego* is the proof of the *subex*.

This is why the experience takes place, simultaneously, in the two antinomic forms of the ego and the union, which are, however, the same experience, prior and subsequent to the distinction between substances. The experience of the *unum quid* is dual, traversed by a contrariety, which introduces within it the act of mediation through which the subject (or the *subex*) secures itself:

> I think it was those meditations rather than the thoughts requiring less attention that have made Your Highness find obscurity in the notion we have of the union of the mind and the body. It does not seem to me that the human mind is capable of forming a very distinct conception of both the distinction between the soul and the body and their union; for to do this it is necessary to conceive them as a single thing and at the same time to conceive them as two things; and this is absurd.[43]

"These meditations" are explicitly those "needed to appreciate the distinction between the mind and the body" (AT III 693/III.227), as the previous sentence remarks, which refers in this way more generally to all the "meditations" that the Princess Elizabeth has taken the time to practice, and hence to the whole trajectory of the *Meditations* up to the proof of the distinction. At that point, then, the trajectory is disrupted. The possibility of thinking the union calls for a kind of inversion of the course of the mediation, or more exactly for the abstention from meditation: "But it is the ordinary course of life and conversation, and abstention from meditation and from the study of the things which exercise the imagination, that teaches us how to conceive the union of the soul and the body" (AT III 692/III.227).

If in doubt I abstain from passing judgment on any truth, I must here abstain from abstaining myself. By inverting the same gesture, I come back to the same point: the interruption of the abstention, to which I am compelled by the extreme point of my feint, which pronounces *ego sum*—here, I must abstain from meditating, and I conceive the union. In both cases, the suspension of the meditating suspense opens onto the position of what is absolutely distinguished insofar as it gives *itself from itself*. And now this human being "is a true *ens per se, and not an ens per accidens.*"[44] As a being that exists from itself, *per se*, but who is not—neither more nor less than *ego sum*—substantivized by its own *per se*, the human being determines as undetermined the unity of the Subject. *Unum quid*: a something that makes up a One without reification, and hence without one*ness*. And something that, for this reason, gives itself twice: as ego, as union.

In giving itself twice, the subject always gives itself—each day, each time, each time I say *I* and each time that I *live*—and never gives *itself*, since there is nothing that can *itself* be posited and grasped. The subject is nothing but the experience of the *unum quid*, and this experience is without object, status, or procedure. The proof of the union of the soul and the body is there less to provide an account of the finalized functionings that I observe in the being that we call human than to point out the being *per se* of the subject as being *per se* of the human being—who supports himself only by supporting himself with nothing. At the outer extremity of doubt as well as in everyday life, Descartes perceived—in the instant of a stroke of diaphragm—that the human being is the Subject, and that within the human being, the Subject infinitely ruins itself and collapses into the abyss.

At this point, thought convulses: It properly reaches what it thinks, it closes a system upon its last certainty—the union of the soul and the body—and because this certainty is *its own self*, it remains there, tied to as much as wrenched from itself, in this double suspension without status where the subject, simultaneously, can no longer doubt nor meditate anymore. Cataleptic and broken *ego* at the same time.

Descartes is the founder neither of humanism nor of anthropology or the so-called human sciences. He made their general program possible only at the cost of a misunderstanding—inevitable, no doubt, and inscribed every-where within his discourse as well—of the impossible experience of the human being that the thinking of the Subject is compelled to reach, but which it cannot face. It is not possible to *face unum quid*, faceless subject or face without substance, convulsive posture of *ego quasi permixtum* to itself, articulating and disarticulating itself in the same gesture, in a gesture that is only a contraction.

"Humanism is opposed," Heidegger writes, "because it does not set the *humanitas* of the human being high enough."[45] In the thinking of the Subject and by means of a convulsive thought, a *humanitas* was thought that remains exorbitant for this humanism to which we still belong—even if against our own *body*.[46]

Ego sum—unum quid: the measure of another *humanitas*, of this diaphrag-med *humanitas* found in Descartes's discourse, cannot be provided by a thinking that pretends to be of the body, or of the absence of subject. It is not even—especially not—a thinking of the subject as a structural, histori-cal, or fictional effect, nor as an effect of the unconscious, the imaginary, or the symbolic. For in one way or another, all these instances impose a topol-ogy of the *substance*: somewhere, in some place, *that* [ça] is supported by something. *Unum quid* supports itself with nothing, and yet it takes place constantly. It does not support itself by uttering itself, since that vanishes at the instant of the uttering, nor by uniting itself with the body, since this union is an *ens per se* in which its self is lost or can only be conceived if it ceases to conceive.

Here, no *measure* should be expected. The incommensurable is what makes possible the *quasi permixtio* of the union, and also what makes of this union an incommensurable thought, exorbitant to thinking itself. In the *quasi permixtio*, thought *is extended*. It is perhaps what Freud sensed when he wrote in a posthumous note: "Psyche is extended, knows nothing about it."[47] Such a thought could only come to Freud because he was thinking against the Cartesian subject. But this thought also "came" to Descartes, and for both Descartes and Freud, this thought falls inexorably outside, in excess of any psycho*analysis*.

The incommensurable extension of thought is the opening of the mouth. The mouth that opens and forms "ego" (other lips had already opened to deliver into the world this "me" when it let out its first cry) is the place of the union insofar as the union is opened and distended, and this is how *unum quid* comes about. This place is not a place, and yet it is not out of place. Within a place, within the extension of a face, it makes up the gaping of a nonplace. In this nonplace the figure (extension, measure) and the figure-lessness (thought without measure) are joined together and distinguished, are joined together through their distinction. The place of the uttering is formed by the internal dis-location of this reunion.

The *psyche* of the Ancients was localized in some organ or other. Aristotle's *psyche*—formal substance of a living body[48]—was united to the body like "the wax and the shape given to it by the stamp." The Cartesian soul (the detailed study of which would show that it carries over many traits of these traditions), as the soul of the one whose being consists in uttering, stands in this place/nonplace of a mouth that opens and closes upon "*ego sum.*" And that opens and closes at once, a second time, repeating and not repeating "*ego existo.*" This double beat utters the subject, utters itself as subject.

But a mouth is neither a substance nor a figure. *Bucca*, a more recent and more trivial term, is not *os*. *Os, oris*, oral mouth, is the face itself taken met-onymically for this mouth that it surrounds, carries, and makes visible, this mouth that is the passageway for all kinds of substances, first of all of this aerial substance of a discourse. *Bucca*, on the other hand, is the puffed cheeks, the movement, the contraction/distention of breathing, eating, spitting, or speaking. Buccality is more primitive than orality. Nothing is yet taking place there, and above all, that has not always-already spoken there. But an unstable and mobile opening forms at the instant of speaking. At this instant, nothing can be discerned; *ego* does not want to say any-thing, *ego* only opens this cavity. Any mouth is a shadowy mouth, and the mouth of the truth also opens onto this darkness, as this darkness, to form its own *for*.

The Freudian child (I will not say subject) is not initiated into an "oral stage." He first opens himself as a mouth, the open mouth of the cry, but also the mouth closed upon the breast to which the child is attached in an identification more ancient than any identification with a figure, as well as the slightly open mouth, detaching itself from the breast, in a first smile or a first facial expression, the future of which is thinking.[49] The mouth is the opening of *Ego, Ego* is the opening of the mouth. What comes to pass there is that ego spaces itself out there. "Clearing-away [*Räumen, espacer*, spacing] brings forth what is free, the open for human's settling and dwelling."[50] But the human being is that which spaces itself out, and which perhaps only ever dwells in this spacing, in the *areality* of his mouth.

> *The buccal space. One of the oddest inventions of the organism. Dwelling of the tongue. Seat of reflexes, of various degrees of persistence. The areas that taste are discontinuous. Multipurpose machinery. There are fountains and furniture.*
>
> *And the bottom of this gulf with its treacherous trapdoors, its snapshots and critical nerviness. Preambles and proclamations. . . .*
>
> *It is a hell-gate of the Ancients.*[51]

The subject ruins itself and collapses into this abyss. But *ego* utters itself there. It externalizes itself there, which does not mean that it carries to the outside the visible face of an invisible interiority. It means, literally, that *ego* makes or makes itself into *exteriority*, spacing of places, distancing and strangeness that make up a place, and hence space itself, primordial spatialiaty of a true *outline* in which, and only in which, *ego* may come forth, trace itself out, and think itself.

It is this thought—*ego, unum quid*—that can alone find out that it does not give rise to any recognition of its subject, of the human being. This thought is always in advance withdrawn from the possibility of recognizing itself, and hence from the possibility of thinking. *Ego* contracts thought to the point where it is wrenched away from itself. It is not a violent act—or it is one to the extent that, from Descartes onward, thought has refused to confront its own convulsion: violence is begotten in what one refuses to confront. But the convulsion of *ego* is not in itself violent—it is neither disorder, nor illness, even though, without doubt, a chaos stirs within it. It is rather the injunction of an ordeal and a task in which could well consist the least improper future of the human being.

PREFACE TO THE ENGLISH EDITION

1. Heidegger, *Contributions to Philosophy: Of the Event* (GA 65), trans. Richard Rojcewicz and Daniela Vallega-Neu (Bloomington: Indiana University Press, 2012), §259, 336.

2. [Usually rendered in English as "the ego." See, for example, Freud's famous paper "*Das Ich und das Es*," which is translated in French as "*Le moi et le ça*" but in English as "The Ego and the Id." (All translator's notes or additions made to existing notes by the translator appear in square brackets.)]

3. [In English in the text followed by the French word "*embrayeur*".]

4. [See AT IXa 27.]

5. See Martin Heidegger, *Being and Time*, trans. John Macquarrie and Edward Robinson (Oxford: Blackwell, 1962), 89, H. 62.

TRANSLATOR'S INTRODUCTION

1. As Nancy and Lacoue-Labarthe write: "even the gap of the *shifter* operates almost as a sort of confirmation of the subject adhering to its own certainty through the certainty of its noncoincidence to itself." Philippe Lacoue-Labarthe and Jean-Luc Nancy, *The Title of the Letter: A Reading of Lacan*, trans. François Raffoul and David Pettigrew (Albany: SUNY Press, 1992), 121.

2. Jacques Derrida, *Writing and Difference*, trans. Alan Bass (Chicago: University of Chicago Press, 1978), 33–34.

3. See *The Inoperative Community*, ed. Peter Connor (Minneapolis: University of Minnesota Press, 1991), 20.

4. About contact/separation, see *Being Singular Plural*, trans. Robert D. Richardson and Anne E. O'Byrne (Stanford: Stanford University Press,

2000), 5, 91, 97. About entanglement/disentanglement, see Nancy's discussion of ipseity in "Eulogy for the Mêlée," in ibid., 145–158.

5. See *The Ground of the Image*, trans. Jeff Fort (New York: Fordham University Press, 2005); "The Look of the Portrait" in *Multiple Arts: The Muses II*, ed. Simon Sparks (Stanford: Stanford University Press, 2006); and, more recently, *L'autre portrait* (Paris: Galilée, 2014).

6. See *Identity: Fragments, Frankness*, trans. François Raffoul (New York: Fordham University Press, 2014), 14 (translation modified).

7. See Ian James, "The Persistence of the Subject: Jean-Luc Nancy," *Paragraph* 25, no. 1 (2002): 125–141. This article is slightly reworked in Chapter 1 of *The Fragmentary Demand: An Introduction to the Philosophy of Jean-Luc Nancy* (Stanford: Stanford University Press, 2006), 49–63.

8. See Marie-Eve Morin, *Jean-Luc Nancy* (Cambridge: Polity, 2012), chapter 5.

9. Jacques Derrida, *On Touching—Jean-Luc Nancy*, trans. Christine Irizarry (Stanford: Stanford University Press, 2005).

10. *Corpus*, trans. Richard A. Rand (New York: Fordham University Press).

11. See "*Mundus est fabula*," 651–653.

12. See *Oxford English Dictionary*, 2nd ed., ed. John Simpson and Edmund Weiner (Oxford: Clarendon Press, 1989).

13. "*Dum Scribo*," trans. Ian McLeod, *Oxford Literary Review* 3, no. 2 (1978): 6–21; "*Larvatus pro Deo*," trans. Daniel E. Brewer, *Glyph* II (1977): 14–36; "*Mundus Est Fabula*," trans. Daniel E. Brewer, *Modern Language Notes* 93, no. 4 (1978): 635–653.

EGO SUM: OPENING

1. See *The Discourse of the Syncope: Logodaedalus*, trans. Saul Anton (Stanford: Stanford University Press, 2008), 1–4, "A Digression on Fashion."

2. Michel Foucault, who invented the concept, provides in his works the best representation of what an *epistēmē* is: it is the anthropological concept of general anthropology. In other words, whatever its operative force and precision, it is not a philosophical concept.

3. Martin Heidegger, *Kant and the Problem of Metaphysics*, trans. Richard Taft, 5th enlarged edition (Bloomington: Indiana University Press, 1997), §43, 164.

4. Because it was philosophical, Bataille's anthropology has not remained fashionable, beyond a short explosion of curiosity . . .

5. Philippe Lacoue-Labarthe, *The Subject of Philosophy*, ed. and trans. Thomas Trezise (Minneapolis: University of Minnesota Press, 1993). About this reference and the others that will follow, current practices (including the

so-called return of favors) necessitate an inopportune comment (that will without a doubt be taken for a denegation): It is not friendship or collaboration to a collective work that dictates the reference, but rather the reverse.

6. See *Discourse of the Syncope*, 15 and 138.

7. *The Correspondence of Walter Benjamin, 1910–1940*, ed. Gershom Scholem and Theodor W. Adorno (Chicago: University of Chicago Press, 1994), Letter to Hugo von Hofmannsthal, 13 January 1924, 229 [translation modified].

8. Gérard Granel, "Préface" to Edmund Husserl, *La crise des sciences européennes et la phénoménologie transcendantale* (Paris: Gallimard, 1976), vii [my translation].

9. Since 1936, year of the first conference on the "mirror stage." See Jacques Lacan, *Écrits: The First Complete Edition in English*, trans. Bruce Fink in collaboration with Héloïse Fink and Russell Grigg (New York: Norton, 2006), 52 and n. 4 on 57.

10. See Jean-Claude Milner, *De la syntaxe à l'interprétation* (Paris: Seuil, 1978) and *For The Love of Language*, trans. Ann Banfield (Basingstoke: Palgrave-Macmillan, 1990), as well as André Green, "Psychanalyse, langage: l'ancien et le nouveau," *Critique* 381 (1979), or earlier, Nicolas Abraham, "The Shell and the Kernel: The Scope and Originality of Freudian Psychoanalysis," originally published in *Critique* 249 (1968) and reprinted in Nicolas Abraham and Marie Torok, *The Shell and the Kernel: Renewals of Psychoanalysis*, trans. Nicholas T. Rand (Chicago: University of Chicago Press, 1994).

11. Jean Petitot-Cocorda, "Sur ce qui revient à la psychose," in *Folle vérité: Vérité et vraisemblance du texte psychotique*, ed. Julia Kristeva and Jean-Michel Ribelles (Paris: Seuil, 1979), 223–269. All the quotations are from 267–268.

12. See, for example, Jean-Michel Ribettes, "Le Phalsus," in *Folle vérité*, 135, or Daniel Sibony, *Le nom et le corps* (Paris: Seuil, 1974), 160 et al.

13. It is for this reason, incidentally, that I take the liberty to make these somewhat repetitive comments, the principle of which appears to me to have been established for many years already.

14. This would then also be related to the general problematic of the *remainder* as it is articulated in several of Jacques Derrida's works, a question which is none other than that of the *beginning* or first *incision* [*l'*entame] of discourse, that is, the question of a certain *writing*, as the psychoanalytical discourse does not fail to come to recognize (see for example Daniel Sibony, *Le nom*, 12, passim). We will not take up for itself the interrogation which is opened by these questions, and which would have to do with a *psychoanalysis that would be written*. Let us only add this other precision: if, in certain of its aspects, what we are saying here about psychoanalysis bears certain analogies with the way in which Cornelius Castoriadis attempts to take the critical

measure of psychoanalysis, our attempts diverge radically when the question is sharpened to the point of its furthest implication. See Cornelius Castoriadis, "Psyche," in *Crossroads in the Labyrinth*, trans. Kate Soper and Martin H. Ryle (Cambridge, Mass.: MIT Press, 1984), 1–115. Castoriadis's demand remains, despite the distrust he shows toward the philosophical critique of psychoanalysis (197), dependent upon the aim of a discourse more powerful, more "capable," or more unitary, than analytical discourse. It is something completely different that must be at stake here, if analysis has already opened, cut into, and hence started to undermine [*entamé, en tous les sens*] such a discourse.

15. I am extending, here again, the analysis of "the undecidable" that was begun in *The Discourse of the Syncope*.

16. Maurice Blanchot, "Le discours philosophique," *L'Arc* 46 "Merleau-Ponty" (1971), reprinted in *La Condition critique: Articles 1945–1998* (Paris: Gallimard, 2010), 332–337, at 332.

17. Ibid., 333.

18. Ibid., 334.

19. Ibid., 336.

20. Theodor W. Adorno, *Negative Dialectics*, trans. E. B. Ashton (London: Routledge, 2004), 15. It must be pointed out that this does not contradict the motif of the literarity or textuality of philosophy; it is rather a matter of sharpening this motif to the point of exhaustion.

21. See François Récanati, *La transparence et l'énonciation* (Paris: Seuil, 1979), 198–199, which testifies to the necessity of inventing a linguistic treatment sui generis for the "cogito."

22. Blanchot, "Le discours philosophique," 337.

23. Admittedly, Lacan was saying, in 1954: "The core of our being does not coincide with the ego. That is the point of the analytic experience, and it is around this that our experience is organized, and around this that these strata of knowledge which are now being taught have been deposited. But do you think that we should be content with that, and say—the *I* of the unconscious subject is not *me* [moi]? That is not good enough because nothing, for those of you who think spontaneously, if one can say that, implies the inverse. And normally you start thinking that the *I* is the real ego. . . . In this way, you have accomplished the decentring essential to the Freudian discovery, but you have immediately reduced it." *The Seminar of Jacques Lacan, Book II: The Ego in Freud's Theory and in the Technique of Psychoanalysis 1954–1955*, ed. Jacques-Alain Miller, trans. Sylvana Tomaselli (Cambridge: Cambridge University Press, 1988), 44. And about that which he summarized by the expression "*I is an other*" Lacan specified: "In some ways, it can already be found on the periphery

of the fundamental Cartesian intuition" (9). (Incidentally, here, as elsewhere, this would clearly show itself is a repetition, with Freud, of the Heidegger of *Being and Time*.) Expressed in a simpler manner, what remains to be thought would be contained under these two headings: (1) *ego* is this other that is also the same; (2) this sameness of the other and the same lies not at the margin, but at the core of the Cartesian intuition.

24. [In his *Lectures on the History of Philosophy*, Hegel wrote, speaking of Descartes and of the beginning of modern philosophy: "Here, we may say, we are at home, and like the mariner after a long voyage in a tempestuous sea, we may now hail the sight of land." See Hegel, *Lectures on the History of Philosophy: Medieval and Modern Philosophy*, trans. E. S. Haldane and F. H. Simson (Lincoln: University of Nebraska Press, 1995), 217. In "Hegel and the Greeks," Heidegger cites this passage and comments: "With this image Hegel means to suggest the following: The '*ego cogito sum*,' the 'I think, I am,' is the solid ground upon which philosophy can settle truly and completely." See Heidegger, *Pathmarks*, ed. William McNeill (Cambridge: Cambridge University Press, 1998), 325. The same passage is also alluded to by Heidegger in the seminar in Le Thor in 1968. See Martin Heidegger, *Four Seminars*, trans. Andrew J. Mitchell and François Raffoul (Bloomington: Indiana University Press, 2012), 27.]

25. [This passage is from *Beilage* XIII, "*Vorwort zur Fortsetzung der 'Krisis'* (Foreword to the Continuation of the *Crisis*)" and does not appear in the English translation of Husserl's *Crisis*. See Husserl, *Die Krisis der Europäischen Wissenschaften und die transzendentale Phänomenologie*, ed. Walter Biemel, 2nd ed. (The Hague: Martinus Nijhoff, 1976), 438.]

26. The text to which our discussion refers as to its true condition of possibility is the one that spreads over many sections of the Nietzsche lectures, that is, the analysis that traces the last form of the Subject—the Will—back to its inauguration in Cartesian subjectivity. See Heidegger, *Nietzsche, Volumes Three and Four*, ed. David F. Krell, trans. F. A. Capuzzi (New York: Harper & Row, 1982). To this text one must also join the analysis of *mathesis* in Heidegger, *What Is a Thing?*, trans. W. B. Barton Jr. and V. Deutsch (South Bend, Ind.: Gateway, 1967), §5f2, 98–108. A passage of this analysis also holds itself on the edge of the gap or spacing of the uttering: "The *sum* is not a consequence of the thinking but vice versa; it is the ground of thinking, the *fundamentum*. In the essence of positing lies the proposition: I posit. That is a proposition which does not depend upon something given beforehand, but only gives to itself what lies within it. In it lies: '*I posit*': I am the one who posits and thinks. This proposition has the peculiarity of first positing that about which it makes an assertion, the *subjectum*" (104).

We propose then to depart from Heidegger according to the law of this gap that actually already opens in his work and as though in spite of him. This means, among other things, that we designate the uttering of *ego* here as "pre-cogitative" only as part of a first, superficial description of our intention, a description that is consistent with the *order of statements* in the *Meditations*. This does not imply, however, that we aim at the position and value (neither an essential nor an existential one) of the *ego* conceived as an autonomous entity, prior to and external to the *cogito*. Quite the contrary, it is in the *cogito* and as *cogito* that the event or the experience of the uttering of *ego* takes place. Or, if one wants, the experience of thought is that of the *uttering*—and reciprocally. (But the analysis will have to complicate this equivalence.) Thus the one who says *ego sum* is *no other* than the one who says *sum certus me esse rem cogitantem* ("I am certain that I am a thinking thing"), at the beginning of the Third Meditation (AT VII 35/II.24).

I also take this opportunity here to add a remark about Jean-Marie Beyssade's book *La philosophie de Descartes* (Paris: Flammarion, 1979). This new overall interpretation of Descartes was published too late for me to be able to take it into account here in a precise manner. Let me simply point out that, to the extent that one of Beyssade's major theses concerns the primacy of thought in the experience of the *ego* (which he relates to the rejection of an intuition of the *cogito* conceived on the model of an immediate and simple intuition, to which he substitutes "the intuition of the relation, which envelops the duration of the deductive movement and brings together more simple elements, such as the notions of thought and existence, or the maxim that *in order to think, one must exist*" [239]), we can only find in these pages support against all kinds of reduction of the *cogito* to any form of immediacy whatsoever (or against any dissociation between the intuitive and the objectivated *cogito*, the critique of which is one of the decisive resources of Beyssade's argument). Further on, we will point out how this author also confirms, and in a corollary way, the necessity of the problematic of the *cogito*'s utterance. These elements by no means provide the terms of an overall agreement with the book. But it is not necessary to discuss the book any further since we do not situate our discussion within the field of an interpretation of Cartesianism, even less an overall interpretation of it. It seems nonetheless strange that it is possible, nowadays, to propose such an interpretation without undertaking any kind of analysis of the Heideggerian reading of Descartes. The lack of engagement with this reading seems even stranger when, voluntarily or not, some of its implications are put into play: thus, in Beyssade, the important motif of thought as "immediate unity . . . of a presentation and a representation" (163 n. 2).

27. Heidegger, *Nietzsche, Volume IV: Nihilism*, 117 [translation modified].

28. [*"Veritas se ipsam patefacit."* See Baruch Spinoza, "Treatise on the Emendation of the Intellect," in *Complete Works*, ed. M. L. Morgan, trans. S. Shirley et al. (Indianapolis: Hackett, 2002), 17.]

29. Gilles Deleuze and Félix Guattari, *Anti-Oedipus: Capitalism and Schizophrenia*, trans. Robert Hurley, Mark Seem, and Helen R. Lane (Minneapolis: University of Minnesota Press, 1983), 8.

30. Friedrich Nietzsche, *Beyond Good and Evil*, trans. Judith Norman (Cambridge: Cambridge University Press, 2002) §17, 17.

31. Heidegger, *Nietzsche, Volume IV: Nihilism*, 146.

32. Ibid., 148.

33. Jacques Derrida, "Cogito and the History of Madness," in *Writing and Difference*, trans. Alan Bass (Chicago: University of Chicago Press, 1978), 57. This text constitutes the second condition of possibility of our remarks. For it is not, again, a matter of "scholarly" debates or of "interpretations" to "decide" that the *cogito* takes place only at the extreme point where thought undecides itself in madness—or, more precisely: at the extreme point where thought *is undecided*, absolutely, and hence includes within itself the possibility, and more than the mere possibility, of madness, just as much as it includes the possibility—and the impossibility—of thought. One only needs, incidentally, to read Descartes. Hence, Jean Petitot-Cocorda, for example, in the text mentioned above, also refers to the same analysis by Derrida. Jean-Marie Beyssade, for his part, gives the references to the discussion between Foucault and Derrida (see 158 n. 4), but this reminder, oddly enough, does not seem to play any role in his argumentation.

34. Even Martial Gueroult, who keeps the term "reflectivity" when speaking of the *cogito*, actually directs his entire analysis toward a reflectivity without reflection, if one can say so, without any redoubling or mediation. See Martial Gueroult, *Descartes' Philosophy Interpreted According to the Order of Reasons. Volume I: The Soul and God*, trans. Roger Ariew (Minneapolis: University of Minnesota Press, 1984), 62. The whole history of the *cogito*, via Spinoza, Kant, Fichte, Hegel, Nietzsche, Husserl, and Lacan has only ever been that of the various, even contradictory, ways of denouncing, avoiding, reflecting, suspending, or mediating the *im*mediacy of the *cogito*. Everything plays itself out here: the "cogito" holds itself only on the limit that is common to an identity (the one attributed to it by Gueroult, whose tight and delicate argumentation demonstrates the difficulty of the problem) and a difference (that between two instances of thought, and/or of a duration of thought, which Beyssade opposes to Gueroult). Beyond the debate about reading

protocols, the common limit is formulated in the Heideggerian context in the following way: "In 'I posit' the 'I' as the positer is co- and pre-posited." See Heidegger, *What Is a Thing?*, 104. Such a limit can no longer have to do either with identity or difference, either with immediacy or mediation. It "concerns" [*relève*] only . . . itself: Descartes exhausted all his energy saying nothing else, and it is in this *same* thing that we must exhaust ourselves. A discourse that interprets, reconstitutes, or grounds again will not be sufficient.

35. To tell the truth (so to speak), this is also not what Spinoza proposes, for the revelation or "patefaction" of the true is not for him a kind of (re) presentation, but as we know, a kind of volition that is enveloped by the idea. Yet this act of volition could very well entail something like an utterance, or rather, withdrawn from any verbalization, something like an "uttering." See the following passage of Spinoza's *Ethics*: "they thus regard ideas as though they were inanimate pictures on a panel, and, filled with this misconception, do not see that an idea, inasmuch as it is an idea, involves an affirmation or negation." Spinoza, *Ethics*, trans. R. H. M. Elwes (Mineola, N.Y.: Dover, 1955), Book II, Prop. XLIX scholium. Those who are mistaken here are obviously the Cartesians. The rejection of the *cogito* conceived as the reflectivity of the (mute) representation would go hand in hand with an essential "self-uttering" of the idea. In other words, would Spinoza not begin to (re)open, beyond the cogito and beyond the mute world of representations, the origin of a "saying (to) oneself" as "telling the truth/ saying the true? But we will not get into this discussion here because it is not the place, and also because it would probably very quickly lead to the necessity of putting into question the will (and hence the subjectity) that is entailed by the affirmation of the idea. On the other hand, it will be possible to note further down (see "*Larvatus pro Deo*") that Descartes's picture is not a mute one.

36. We would thus gladly—be it only for the pleasure of strategy—turn into a Cartesian argument the Anglo-Saxon critique of Cartesianism, first in its behaviorist form, and then in the form of the theory of automata. See in this regard the clarification sketched by Francis Jacques in his preface to the French translation of Ryle's *The Concept of Mind* (*La notion d'esprit*, trad. Stern-Gillet [Paris: Payot, 1978]).

37. See "Lapsus judicii," in *A Finite Thinking*, ed. Simon Sparks (Stanford: Stanford University Press, 2003). The concept of "areality" arises out of an analysis of the "subject of right," which in turn opens onto the problematic of the categorical imperative. This group of questions has as its horizon the elaboration of the more general figure of the *syncope*, which it is a matter here of providing with its unavoidable Cartesian premises.

1. [AT X 414/I.41. All references to the *Rules* appear in parentheses and are always to AT X, followed by Volume I of the *Complete Works*. The translation has been adjusted when required by Nancy's usage.]

2. [Cottingham often renders *scientia* as science, but in this context also sometimes as knowledge. See II.10 n. 1. Here I have rendered *scientia* as science in order to differentiate it from *savoir*, which is rendered as knowing or knowledge, depending on the context.]

3. [AT I 137–138/III.23. As a footnote to the passage notes, the larger project mentioned is probably *The World*. The original reads "them," i.e., "some other treatises I began while I was in Paris."]

4. [*Discourse, Part Six*, AT VI 61–62/I.142–143.]

5. [Second Meditation, AT VII 24/II.16.]

6. [Adrien Baillet, *La Vie de Monsieur Des-Cartes, Volume II* (Paris: Horthemels, 1691), Book VII, Chapter XXII, 428.]

7. [See AT VI 66/I.145.]

8. [*Discourse*, AT VI 65–66/I.144–145.]

9. [*The Search for Truth*, AT X 497–498/II.401.]

10. [Second Meditation, AT VII 30/II.20; translation modified.]

11. [Ibid., 31/21.]

12. [See Rule Three, where the imagination is said to "botch things together (*male componentis*)" (368/14).]

13. [A calamus is an ancient reed pen. The allusion might be to Blaise Pascal's famous *Pensées* §347: "Man is but a reed, the most feeble thing in nature; but he is a thinking reed. The entire universe need not arm itself to crush him. A vapour, a drop of water suffices to kill him. But, if the universe were to crush him, man would still be more noble than that which killed him, because he knows that he dies and the advantage which the universe has over him; the universe knows nothing of this" in Pascal, *Pensées*, trans. W. F. Trotter (New York: Dutton, 1958).]

14. [The passage in question is the following: "*si peut-être leur imagination est assez extravagante pour inventer quelque chose de si nouveau*" (IXa 15). The English translation follows the Latin more closely: "if perhaps they manage to think up something so new" (AT VII 20/II.13). Elsewhere in the *Meditations*, *excogitare* is translated as "think up" (AT VII 64/II.45) or "*former en mon esprit*" (IXa 51); "think" (AT VII 68/II.47) or "*concevoir*" (IXa 54), and "devise" (AT VII 87/II.60) or "*imaginer*" (IXa 69).]

15. [Second Meditation, AT VII 32/II.22.]

16. [The reference is to Montaigne's "Apology for Raymond Sebond," Book II §12 of the *Essays*. There we can read: "We cannot worthily conceive

the grandeur of those sublime and divine promises, if we can conceive them at all; to imagine them worthily, we must imagine them unimaginable, ineffable, and incomprehensible." See *The Complete Essays of Montaigne*, trans. Donald Murdoch Frame (Stanford: Stanford University Press, 1958), 385.]

17. [*Principles of Philosophy*, Part Four §197, AT VIIIa 320–321/I.284.]

LARVATUS PRO DEO

1. Regarding the manipulation that gives rise to the title of this essay, I found out that it had already been used by Léon Brunschvicg, with very different intentions (in "Métaphysique et mathématique chez Descartes," *Revue de métaphysique* [1927], 323). This acknowledgment might suffice to remove any misgiving in the reader who would suspect an intemperate modernity in the wordplay.

2. One only has to glance through the literature on Descartes to find these various adventures. One can recall, above all, Maxime Leroy's book *Descartes le philosophe au masque*, in two volumes (Paris, 1929), and, concerning the "Preliminaries," the commentaries by Adam and Tannery, by H. Gouhier (*Les premières pensées de Descartes* [Paris, 1958]), by J. Sirven (*Les Années d'apprentissage de Descartes* [Paris, 1928]), as well as the book *Descartes par lui-même* by S. de Sacy (Paris, 1956).

3. Descartes, "Preliminaries," in *Early Writings*, AT X 213/I.2.

4. "He who hides well, lives well" (Ovid, *Tristia*, Book III, section 4, line 25). Cf. Descartes's Letter to Mersenne, April 1634. [Less literal translations of Ovid include "A low profile means good fortune," "who lives quietly lives well," or as in the translation of Descartes's Letter: "to live well you must live unseen." Cf. AT I 286/III.43.]

5. Hence, in general the *narrative* mode of Cartesian exposition, the specificity of which Hegel strongly emphasizes in his *History of Philosophy*. We will come back to it (see *"Mundus Est Fabula"* in this volume). However, it should already be pointed out that this mode, which is closely related to the pictorial model, concerns the three foundational texts of Cartesian philosophy: the *Regulae*, the *Discourse*, and the *Meditations* (and, in a more limited way *The World* and the *Treatise on Man*). (As for the *Principles*, they are an exposition designed for the schools—or so the author desired; it is not surprising that the pedagogical intention suffices to dismantle the most proper exposition of a thinking.)

6. Letter to Beeckman, October 17, 1630. [This part of the letter is not translated in Cottingham. The original reads: *"Propono tibi ob oculos aliquem caecum, qui sic ex avaritia insaniret, ut totos dies inter alienarum aedium purgamenta quaereret gemmas, et quotiescunque glareola aliqua vel vitri fragmentum*

sub manus ejus incideret, protinus aestimaret esse lapidem valde pretiosum" (AT I 161–162).]

7. Letter to Mersenne, October 8, 1629 (AT I 23/III.6).

8. What is at issue here is not—or not only—Descartes's "psychology," but also his doctrine. How could he have confidence in frankness since he has just invented, on his own, frankness as a method, that is, the very conditions of veracity?

9. *Optics*, AT VI 81/I.152.

10. More generally, one should examine all the procedures of comparison, metaphors, or modeling whereby Cartesian light is always presented as the object of *indirect* sight.

11. The importance of this determination is also noted by J.-M. Beyssade, *La philosophie première*, 234: "I see, and what is indubitable is only that I seem to see. Is it that sensation is dubitable and only reflective thought indubitable? Not at all: What is indubitable within thought is the pure appearing insofar as it rules out all construction, all distance between two terms, all position by a judgment of a separate reality of the appearing."

12. I owe all information concerning Apelles to the exemplary documentation collected by Dominique Bergougnan throughout the *Enciclopedia dell'arte classica e orientale* (Rome: Istituto della Enciclopedia Italiana, 1958–73); August Pauly's *Realencyclopädie der Classischen Altertumwissenschaft* (Stuttgart: J. B. Metzler, 1894–1980) [the updated version, *Des neue Pauly*, is available in English as the *Brill's New Pauly: Encyclopaedia of the Ancient World* (Leiden: Brill, 2006–)]; Emmanuel Bénézit's *Dictionnaire des peintres, sculpteurs, dessinateurs et graveurs* (Paris: Gründ, 1948) [trans. as *The Benezit Dictionary of Artists* (Paris: Gründ, 2006)]; and Louis Houticq's *Encyclopédie des Beaux-Arts* (Paris: Hachette, 1925).

13. Rule Four, AT X 374/I.17.

14. [Nancy is referring to Derrida's 1963 essay "Cogito and the History of Madness," published in *Writing and Difference* (Chicago: University of Chicago Press, 1978), where Derrida takes up Foucault's 1961 *Folie et déraison: Histoire de la folie à l'âge classique* (Paris: Plon, 1961), expanded in 1971. The expanded version is translated into English by Jonathan Murphy and Jean Khalfa as *History of Madness* (London: Routledge, 2006). This edition includes Foucault's 1972 response to Derrida, "My Body, This Paper, This Fire" (550–574). The difference between the French and the Latin text of the passage in question here is discussed on page 561.]

15. It is true that the episode of colors precedes the Evil Genius, whose intervention makes even colors dubitable. But it is here only a matter of pointing out the relation between color and figure as such.

16. One should open up the gap formed here by the correspondence between the theoretical apparatus and the conjuncture, both of which force the author to conceal himself. This conjuncture is that of the Galileo affair—Galileo who later will have *lost his sight* when Descartes will wish to have him read his works.

17. [Nancy says "second," but the passage quoted is found in the Third Meditation.]

18. [The English follows the Latin *statuarius sibi simile signum exculpsit*, while the French, which Nancy uses, speaks of a picture rather than a statue.]

19. The confession, however, dissimulates in turn another proposition, which is to be analyzed in the next part of this work (*"Mundus Est Fabula"*), namely, that only the fictitious creation of another possible world provides, in accordance with the demands of certainty, the true science of our world. The theoretical status of fiction, such as it governs all of modern science, is thereby instituted.

20. It must at least be recalled, briefly, that the *cogito* makes known *that there is* a substance, that is a *subject* of the operation, but not—in the moment of the cogito itself—*what* this substance is. The knowledge of the *cogito* itself, strictly limited to what constitutes it as such, is but the knowledge of a something as subject, that is, as well, of a subject as something that *nothing*, in this *instant*, yet determines either as "consciousness" or even as "thought" in any determinate meaning of the term. In the instant of the cogito, *thinking* [le penser] is but the self-positioning of the fictioning operation of doubt, which substantiates itself at the tip of its feint. It substantiates itself, or according to the following passage of the Replies to Hobbes, "materializes" itself: "It may be that the subject of any act can be understood only in terms of a substance (or even, if he insists, in terms of 'matter', i.e. metaphysical matter)" (AT VII 175/II.124). Insofar as the word "matter"—with and despite Descartes's precautions—designates something here (and is not merely equivalent to "something" in the sense of "whatever"), it must denote what evades all assignation and designation: the subject's formlessness and namelessness, who indeed here has no form at all, and cannot be named *since its pure nomination is equivalent to its self-utterance, which utters only the act of self-uttering* . . . Here, pure anonymity (which we will discuss later) and pure identity are rigorously the same "thing."

21. To Mersenne, December 23, 1630 (AT I 194/III.29).

22. Letter to Chanut, November 1, 1646: "Him doth a painful death await/Who, known too well by all, too late/To know himself doth meet his fate" (AT IV 537/III.300). [The reference is to Seneca, *Thyestes*, 400. In the

translation by F. J. Miller, the passage reads: "On him does death lie heavily, who, but too well known to all, dies to himself unknown."]

23. This will later have to be extended through an analysis of the peculiar exemplarity put into play by the *fable* of the *Discourse*.

24. This is why only anonymity will do here, and not a pseudonymity such as that of Polybius, citizen of the world.

25. Letter to Mersenne, February 27, 1637 (AT I 351/III.54).

26. See Voetius's text, cited by Descartes in his letter to him: "his name, for a while kept secret, and which he himself revealed, is René Descartes [*Nomen illi ad tempus silentio pressum, et ab eo ipso indicatum est* Renato des Cartes]" (AT VIIIb 21). If it were not superfluous, one might add to this discussion the analysis of the feint, through which Descartes presents his *Discourse* as a response to a false rumor that he had a philosophy. He pretends, then, that he has indeed forged himself one so that the false rumor ceases to be false; the argument thus reproduces the procedure that lets truth arise out of falsehood, this time, undoubtedly, with a scarcely concealed irony, yet one that might unveil the constant irony that governs this procedure throughout the *Discourse*, as if certainty was only certain of the fact that it is feigning to be certain . . . (see AT VII 30–31/I.136).

27. [This is how Bossuet, following Tertullian, speaks of the corpse in his *Funeral Oration for Henrietta of England*. See also Nancy, *Corpus*, 59–61.]

28. [The addition in parentheses is not found word for word in this passage from the *Discourse*.]

29. This will clearly have to be established by examining the fable of the *cogito*.

30. Erwin Panofsky, *Perspective as Symbolic Form*, trans. Christopher S. Wood (New York: Zone Books, 1991), 70. Panofsky's entire book would require a commentary along the line of the Cartesian motif.

31. Ibid., 29.

32. Sigmund Freud, *The Standard Edition of the Complete Psychological Works of Sigmund Freud*, Vol. 8, *Jokes and Their Relation to the Unconscious* (London: Hogarth Press, 1960), 59.

33. [Discourse Three, on the eye, is omitted from *The Philosophical Writings*. For the quoted passage, see Descartes, *Discourse on Method, Optics, Geometry and Meteorology*, trans. P. J. Olscamp (Indianapolis: Bobbs-Merrill, 1965), 85.] This hole opens, of course, onto the darkroom and the problematic proper to it (see Sarah Kofman, *Camera Obscura: Of Ideology*, trans. Will Straw [Ithaca, N.Y.: Cornell University Press, 1998]). For this reason, the hole has the structure of the diaphragm, which will be discussed later (see "*Unum Quid*").

34. We know that masks were used for reasons of modesty, for example in the doorless latrines of certain Venetian homes of the Renaissance. During the Elizabethan period, masks were also worn at the theater by noble ladies, and we will see later that a masked woman viewer is appropriate to the spectacle presented by Descartes.

35. It would be even more pertinent to examine the plays of Jesuit theater from this period, such as the *Cenodoxus* by Bidermann, a story of hypocrisy and feint, where Death repeats, as in Calderón, that "life is a dream." One would then have to examine this moral theater designed to support a morality of life, where life itself is conceived of as a theater, a morality we find in Descartes. (See, for example, Letter to Elizabeth, May 18, 1645.) [AT IV 202–203.]

36. See Adrien Baillet, *La Vie de Monsieur Descartes*, Vol. II (Paris, Horthenels, 1861), 407. Cited at AT XI 661.

37. Ibid., 408.

38. Cited at AT XI 661–662.

39. Sándor Ferenczi, *Thalassa: A Theory of Genitality*, trans. Henry Alden Bunker (New York: Norton, [1924] 1968), 14.

40. Second Meditation, AT VII 26/II.17.

41. [*Personne*, from the Latin *persona*, theater mask.]

42. Paul Valéry, *Cahiers/Notebooks 5*, trans. and ed. Brian Stimpson, Paul Gifford, Robert Pickering, and Norma Rinsler (Frankfurt: Peter Lang, 2010), 237.

43. Alain (Émile Chartier), "Éloge de Descartes," *Éléments de philosophie*, vol. II, Chapter 10. I would also like to add to this entire text another reference, which should have been fundamental to it if it had not been discovered after the fact. It is the essay by Michel Beaujour titled "Autobiographie et autoportrait," published in *Poétique* 32 (Nov. 1977): 442–458 [translated into English as the Introduction to *Poetics of the Literary Self-Portrait* (New York: NYU Press, 1992), 1–21]. Beaujour distinguishes under the name of *self-portrait* a literary category the essential characteristics of which seem to overlap exactly with those brought to light by the pictorial model found in Descartes's texts. Allow me to cite only the most prominent of these characteristics: "The self-portrait lays its cards on the table: its secret lies in that obviousness" (10). Even though Beaujour takes at least one of his examples from Descartes, he holds that the Cartesian *cogito* "fills up" and "censures" (13) the impossible experience of writing oneself he calls self-portrait: such have been undoubtedly the ideological effects of the *cogito*, but such is not the functioning of its *Discourse*, the nature of which as "self-portrait" (so to speak, and if it is possible to condense without betraying too much: the endless writing of a

subject in excess over himself) appears, as far as I am concerned, to be confirmed by Beaujour's analyses, however different they are from mine.

1. *The Complete Fables of La Fontaine: A New Translation in Verse*, trans. Craig Hill (New York: Arcade Publishing, 2011), xxxv.

2. Until we speak again of the soul and the body in the next chapter. See "*Unum Quid.*"

3. [See "*Ego Sum*" in this volume.]

4. [*Immonde* means base, vile, or foul and is used to describe, for example, an appalling crime, a filthy street, or a foul smell. In *The Creation of the World*, Nancy will make ample use of the term "*immonde*" to describe the contemporary world of globalization, which is an unworld also in the literal sense of the word: a world that does quite succeed in making a world.]

5. Let us recall that Descartes specified, earlier in the Third Meditation, the meaning of the words "objective" (the reality of the object in my mind) and "formal" (which is equivalent to "actual" or "real," that is, to the reality of the thing existing in itself).

6. Translation of the French AT IXa 63–64. The English and Latin version are different. See AT VII 80/II.55–56: "Despite the high degree of doubt and uncertainty involved here, the very fact that God is not a deceiver, and the consequent impossibility of there being any falsity in my opinions which cannot be corrected by some other faculty supplied by God offers me a sure hope that I can attain the truth even in these matters [i.e., particular or less clearly understood aspects of corporeal things, such as light, sound, or pain]."

7. See "*Larvatus pro Deo*" in this volume.

8. [See AT X 423/I.47. The English reads: "for example when we take as gospel truth a story which someone has told us."]

9. [See Rule Four, AT X 374/I.17.]

10. AT XI 32–33/I.90.

11. [The verb "*feindre*" appears many times in Chapter VI of *The World* and is translated as "fashioning," "imagining," "pretending," or "making up." See AT XI 33–36/I.90–92.]

12. This is the foundation of the scientificity of the modern sciences, the very functioning of which Descartes thinks in the following way: from the invention of the fable (theory) to the institution of experiment (the instrumental construction of a fabulous machine), we do not go from a "hypothesis" to testing it against the facts, but rather we put the subject to work, this subject who is indistinguishable from his operation as artist-technician.

13. Le Bossu, *Treatise of the epick poem*, trans. W.J. (London: Thomas
Bennet: 1695) [originally published in French in 1675]. Nancy cites Áron
Kibédi-Varga, "L'invention de la fable," *Poétique* 25 (1976): 107–115, here
110–111. [The addition in parentheses is from the latter text and not found in
the original treatise.] Incidentally, it is noticeable how much Nietzsche's
Zarathustra still answers to this same philosophical poetic.

14. In what follows, we rely on the monumental commentary by Etienne
Gilson: *René Descartes, Discours de la méthode: texte et commentaire*, 3ʳᵈ ed.
(Paris: Vrin, 1962).

15. Which is to say, one of the questions that should be raised here is the
following: In any attempt to blur the distinction between truth (or theory)
and fiction, or even any attempt to identify them in any way whatsoever (and
there exist many, from the Romantics to Nietzsche up to the present), at one
moment or another, and whether we want it or not, the question must be
raised whether and to what extend such an attempt is fundamentally dependent
on Descartes.

16. The various possible exploitations of this hypothesis are no doubt so
easily surmised that we might be excused if we disregard them here. In any
case, it will not be a matter of arriving at either one or many figures of the
subject of the Discourse: It is the subject prior to every figure—or the figure
before every subject.

17. Here I transpose the free will [*franc-arbitre*] found elsewhere in
Descartes or free subject [*franc-sujet*] of a political theoretician like Jean
Bodin. [Nancy probably has in mind the *libre arbitre* of *The Principles of
Philosophy*. The term *franc-arbitre* is, as far as I know, not found in Descartes's
works. The reference to Bodin is to the *Six Books of the Commonwealth*, Book I,
Chapters VI–VII.]

18. Descartes's frankness and dissimulation are exposed with equal evidence
if we recall this letter that he received from Balzac in 1628: "Moreover, Sir,
please remember the story of your mind. All of our friends await it and you
promised it to me in front of Father Clitophon. . . . I will take pleasure in
reading your various adventures in the middle and the uppermost ethereal
region, in considering your prowess against the Scholastic Giants, the path to
which you have held and the progress you have made in the truth of things"
(AT I 570–571). The kinship that is suggested here between Don Quixote and
Descartes should be studied for itself: *Don Quixote* is also the fable of fabulation.

19. Undoubtedly, any autobiographical project must proceed from the
Cartesian model, be it modified into Rousseau's and then Proust's. But it
would be important to show how, on the other hand, the Cartesian model
depends closely upon Montaigne's.

20. The "two types of minds," as the rest of the passage explains, are those who precipitate judgments and those who follow the opinions of others. Those, then, who have not recognized the Method. And as we read in the passage, the world is largely composed of them. There remains—almost—only I.

21. *Author's Replies to the Sixth Set of Objections* (AT VII 423/II.285). Unlike the *Method*, such a knowledge or science could and should be able to *be taught*.

22. See Rudolf Boehm, *Das Grundlegende und das Wesentliche: Zu Aristoteles' Abhandlung 'Über das Sein und das Seiende' (Metaphysik Z)* (The Hague: M. Nijhoff, 1965), §31, 201. [Nancy is quoting from E. Martineau's translation. The original reads: "*das Wesen [würde] gleichsam durch die Entdeckung seiner selbst verborgen.*" A more literal rendering of the original would be "the essence would almost be concealed over by its own uncovering"].

23. The Second Meditation will proceed according to the feint's (inseparable) reverse side: "But there is a deceiver of supreme power and cunning who is deliberately and constantly deceiving me. In that case I too undoubtedly exist, if he is deceiving me" (AT VII 25/II.17). Therefore, *I am tricked* [feinté], and I am tricked by my *fiction* of an Evil Genius. [Note that Nancy misquotes the French text of the *Replies to the Sixth Set of Objections*. It reads *sorte de connaissance* and not *force*. See IXa 225].

24. In a letter dated July 13, 1638 (to Morin, AT II 209–210), Descartes remarks that being and reason are contemporaneous, like light-*lux* and light-*lumen*, the former being the cause of the latter. See on this M. Gueroult, *Descartes' Philosophy Interpreted According to the Order of Reasons, Volume I, The Soul and God*, trans. Roger Ariew (Minneapolis: University of Minnesota Press, 1984), 287 n. 2.

25. Once again, after the *Meditations*, this will be the formula used in the didactic account of the *Principles*. But the didactic account excludes, by definition, the exposition of *invention* (and hence narration), which nevertheless constitutes in Descartes *everything* that there is to expose as far as truth is concerned . . . In ruling out reasoning, we do not come back to an intuitive conception of the *cogito*. It should be understood, with all that has been said above, that the *cogito*—or at least "cogito"—stands in withdrawal and in excess of intuition and reasoning understood together. Therefore, its structure is neither mediate nor immediate. Consequently, if we undoubtedly progress in the characterization of this structure when we identify within it an internal doubling, as J.-M. Beyssade does, some of whose indications we have pointed out, we cannot be content with its characterization as the intuition of a reasoning (be it of another kind than a syllogism). Or we must admit that this way of speaking only names the problem, which is that of the simultaneous

impertinence of the concepts of intuition and reasoning. The same applies to the relation of the *cogito* to time: The *cogito* is undoubtedly neither instantaneous nor diachronic. In every case, it poses the question of what, being neither simple nor double, makes it so that neither unity nor duality can take place *as such*, simply—and that maybe nothing, in any case no "subject," can ever take place *as such*, if not by withdrawing from itself.

26. "Analytic Philosophy and Language" in *Problems of General Linguistics*, trans. Mary Elizabeth Meek (Miami: University of Miami Press, 1971), 1:236. Benveniste had also posited the linguistic principle of what we are trying to analyze here. In "Subjectivity and Language" (published originally, it should be recalled, in 1958), he writes: "It is in and through language that man constitutes himself as a *subject*, because language alone establishes the concept of 'ego' in reality, in *its* reality which is that of the being."

The "subjectivity" we are discussing here is the capacity of the speaker to posit himself as "subject." It is defined not by the feeling which everyone experiences of being himself (this feeling, to the degree that it can be taken note of, is only a reflection) but as the psychic unity that transcends the totality of the actual experiences it assembles and that makes the permanence of the consciousness. Now we hold that that "subjectivity," whether it is placed in phenomenology or in psychology, as one may wish, is only the emergence in the being of a fundamental property of language. "Ego" is he who *says* "ego." That is where we see the foundation of "subjectivity," which is determined by the linguistic status of "person" (224).

Such a "status," or its nonstatutory character, so to speak, is precisely what remains to be interrogated.

An analogous recourse to the performative in relation to the *cogito* can be found in J.-M. Beyssade (*La philosophie première*, 250–251), who concludes: "Far from referring to a tacit *Cogito* behind the garment of the words, Descartes lets the moment of articulation emerge as an autonomous moment, which has in the order of reasons a truth independent of the consequences that will follow and independent also of the singularity, of the actual experience of a given individual at such and such a moment, since it is the truth of an articulation, the opportunity for which is always given in any aspect of a continuing experience" (251). However, if such an "opportunity" is always possible (something that cannot be affirmed without further examination), articulation or performation, and hence the "truth" of this articulation, remain nevertheless inseparable, each time, from the singularity of its event. In turn, the singularity (of the moment, the place, and the subject) only takes place through and within the articulation. The "autonomy" of articulation refers, then, neither to uniqueness nor to permanence. It is therefore insufficient to settle upon a "truth of articulation," and we must instead penetrate into the truth *as* articulation.

27. Hence, we can say that the famous Lacanian prosopopoeia of truth: "I, truth, speak . . ." provides the exact formula of the *cogito* (and in close proximity with all the motifs recalled in the preceding footnote). In the end, this assignation of truth to the identity of the statement and the utterance (the *truth* being therefore *the one who utters*) accomplishes in the most rigorous way the metaphysical program opened by Fichte's repetition of Descartes. Indeed, Fichte writes: "But because the subject of this proposition ['I am I'] is the absolute subject, the subject purely and simply, the (in this single case) the proposition's inner content is posited along with its form." Johann Gottlieb Fichte, "Concerning the Concept of the *Wissenschaftlehre*," in *Early Philosophical Writings*, trans. Daniel Breazeale (Ithaca, N.Y.: Cornell University Press, 1988), 124–125 (*Sämtliche Werke* 1:69). But because of its very exactitude, the exact formula of the *cogito* undoubtedly misses what happens to "cogito"— namely, that as a result, it withdraws. The logic of withdrawal, however, obeys completely different laws then the laws of a "splitting of the subject" as posited by Lacan. The principle of the difference is the following: splitting occurs to the Lacanian subject from the Other, from the Law of the symbolic that constitutes him by dividing him. In this way the veritable Subject of the subject (truth) is identified as "Other" (or, later, as "language"), while at the same time a discourse that masters this identity (that of psychoanalysis) happens to be authenticated. But *in truth*, if I may say so, the subject of "cogito" withdraws *himself*. He is not split; nothing comes to him from any other (even though everything undoubtedly comes to him from the other [*autrui*], but this is a different story), and it is at the height of his being-through-himself-for-himself that he withdraws: he excludes himself, exceeds himself, undecides his sameness, shelters himself too, and defends himself, and protects himself, and cuts himself off, that is, at the same time, mutilates and betrays himself, and collapses. No discourse can master this operation's (or this accident's) relation-to-self, since every discourse is derived from it. No analysis can address itself to the *himself* of the "withdraws himself" except if what addresses *itself* there withdraws *itself* at the same time. The question—raised in relation to any discourse—is finally that of knowing what is privileged in the withdrawal: the dispositive of protection, or the risk of loss. Perhaps even more, what remains to be learned and to be thought is that nothing ought to be privileged. One must not want anything in order to want that it happens.

28. François Recanati, *La transparence et l'énonciation: Pour introduire à la pragmatique* (Paris: Seuil, 1979). [Recanati also published in 1981 an

introduction to performative utterances, translated into English as *Meaning and Force: The Pragmatics of Performative Utterances* (Cambridge: Cambridge University Press, 1987)].

29. In relation to the motif of meaning or wanting to say [*vouloir dire*], the reference to Jacques Derrida's *Voice and Phenomenon* [trans. Leonard Lawlor (Evanston, Ill.: Northwestern University Press, 2011)] is "self"-evident. It is more peculiar, on the other hand, that we are led to raise the question of another possible, apparently fortuitous, reference: does the *for* that we are soliciting here have anything to do with all the *fors* put into play by the same (?) Derrida in relation to the question of a "cryptic" unconscious? See "Fors," Foreword to Nicolas Abraham and Maria Torok, *The Wolf Man's Magic Word: A Cryptonymy* (Minneapolis: University of Minnesota Press, 1986). [As Barbara Johnson, the translator of Derrida's foreword, notes, "The word *fors* in French, derived from the Latin *foris* ('outside, outdoors'), is an archaic preposition meaning 'except for, barring, save.' In addition, *fors* is the plural of the word *for*, which, in the French expression *le for intérieur*, designates the inner heart, 'the tribunal of conscience,' subjective interiority" (xi–xii). Of course, in Nancy's text, *for* is the first person singular of the indicative present of the verb *fari*, to say, to speak.] It might only be the case of a simple homophonic encounter; but something else could also be at stake in this homo(?)phony(?).

30. [The first quotation is attributed to Louis XIV, the second was Victor Hugo's motto, the third is a remark by Gustave Flaubert, the author of *Madame Bovary*, and the last one is found in Stendhal, *The Red and the Black*, Book II, Chapter 28.]

31. Descartes, *The Search for Truth by Means of the Natural Light*, AT X 515/II.540.

UNUM QUID

1. We refer one last time to the last chapters of Martial Gueroult's *Descartes' Philosophy Interpreted According to the Order of Reasons*, trans. Roger Ariew (Minneapolis: University of Minnesota Press, 1985). [Nancy is probably referring to Chapters XII–XVIII in Volume 2, *The Soul and the Body*.]

2. [In the English translation, which follows the Latin text, *quasi* corresponds to "as it were," which modifies *permixtio*. In the French text, however, *quasi* corresponds to "*comme*" in "*je compose comme un seul tout avec lui,*" "I compose something like a unity with it." See AT IXa 64.]

3. The expression *unum quid* appears again in the Synopsis of the Meditations, AT VII 15/II.11.

4. Gueroult, *Descartes' Philosophy*, Volume 2: *The Soul and the Body*, 121.

5. Ibid. It is not without interest to point out that for Malebranche we are "led to believe"—falsely—in the substantial union as a result of original sin, which "has so strengthened our soul's original union with our body that it seems to us that these two parts of us are but one and the same substance" (expression that forces the letter if not the spirit of Descartes's texts, as we will see), while the same sin in contrast "has so weakened our mind's union with God that it can be felt only by those whose heart is purified and whose mind is enlightened" (*The Search After Truth*, ed. and trans. Thomas M. Lennon and Paul J. Olscamp [Cambridge: Cambridge University Press, 1997], xxxiv). Not only is Descartes far from mixing sin with the union, but he also considers that the union brings a specific kind of joy to the soul (of course, sin might lie in this joy): "I think that the soul's first passion was joy, because it is not credible that the soul was put into the body at a time when the body was not in a good condition; and a good condition of the body naturally gives us joy" (Letter to Chanut, 1 February 1647, AT IV 604–605/III.307). We will not develop the theme, sufficiently explicit, of this orgasm. Besides, let us recall, even though it is well known, that Leibniz and Spinoza, obviously for very different reasons, both reject Descartes's substantial union (see for example Leibniz's *Theodicy*, §59 ff. and Spinoza's *Ethics*, Part V, Preface). In any case, the union appeared to the "Cartesians" as the most fragile piece, or the least intelligible notion, of the system. But this criticism cannot be separated—at least this is what ought to be shown—from the rejection, in one form or another, of the *cogito*.

6. Descartes affirms it many times. See, for example, the *Replies to the Second Set of Objections*: "You go on to ask how I demonstrate that a body is incapable of thinking. You will forgive me if I reply that I have as yet provided no opportunity for this question to be raised. I first dealt with the matter in the Sixth Meditation" (AT VII 131/II.94–95).

7. The most elaborate form of such an interpretation is found in Jean Laporte, *Le rationalisme de Descartes* (Paris: Presses Universitaires de France, 1945) and precisely with regard to the substantial union.

8. Descartes specifies it again in 1642 in a letter to P. Gibieuf (dated January 19), and in the middle of a demonstration of the necessary distinction between the soul and the body because of the "complete" idea I have of each. But this completeness corresponds only to the fact that "I can conceive them apart" from one another, and does not imply the exhaustion of the properties of each. Indeed: "But I do not on that account deny that there can be in the soul or the body many properties of which I have no ideas" (AT III 478/III.213). We will see that, ultimately, one of these unknown properties could be an extended nature of the soul . . .

9. "He learns it from experiencing in his own case that it is impossible that he should think without existing" and this is "a simple intuition of the mind" (*Replies to the Second Set of Objections*, AT VII 140/II.100).

10. See the passage that corresponds to this moment of the procedure in *The Search for Truth by Means of the Natural Light* (the date of composition of the dialogue is debated): "Indeed, I do not even know whether I have a body; you have shown me that it is possible to doubt it. I might add that I cannot deny absolutely that I have a body" (AT X 518/II.412).

11. The title of this Meditation announces it (*The existence of material things, and the real distinction between mind and body of man*), but does not let us anticipate the demonstration of the union, the concept of which is nevertheless contained in the notion of *man*.

12. I briefly outline these three traits here and refer globally to almost all of the *Replies to the Objections*, through which we could follow their numerous iterations and variations.

13. As well as that of the "Arguments . . . arranged in geometrical fashion" at the end of the *Replies to the Second Set of Objections* (AT VII 160–170/II. 113–120).

14. This is confirmed by the fact that Descartes always concedes that it is possible that God has created the soul *mortal*.

15. Or, if one wants, as "existing substance," as the text of the *Replies to the Fifth Set of Objections* says, a text that rules out precisely that this leads to any immediate determination with regard to the corporeal nature of the mind (AT VII 386/II.265).

16. See the Sixth Meditation. [Nancy writes "*la distinction 'entière et véritable,*'" which refers to the following passage in the French *Meditations*: "*mon âme . . . est entièrement et véritablement distincte de mon corps*" (AT IXa 62). The English, which translates the Latin, says: "it is certain that I am really distinct from my body [*certum est a corpore meo revera esse distinctum*]" (AT VII 78/II.54).]

17. [This clause does not appear in the Latin version and was added in the French translation by Duc de Luynes in 1642. See AT IXa 47/II.54 n 3.]

18. [As the English states. Emphasis added by Nancy.]

19. [The OED defines syllepsis as "a figure by which a word, or a particular form or inflection of a word, is made to refer to two or more other words in the same sentence, while properly applying to or agreeing with only one of them, or applying to them in different senses."] It must be pointed out that, from a strictly historical point of view, syllepses are much more natural for a seventeenth-century reader, who does not know a syntax as rigid as ours, and who is used to making the verb agree with the closest subject in Latin. This

reader hears, rather: "It is certain that I, that is, that my soul . . ." Nevertheless, the syllepsis between the two concepts remains.

20. It is also through an addition in the French text that Descartes clarifies a couple of lines earlier: "*je suis une chose qui pense*, ou une substance dont toute l'essence ou la nature n'est que de penser [I am a thing that thinks, *or a substance the whole essence or nature of which is only to think*]" (addition underlined, J.-L. N.). [This addition does not appear in the footnotes to the English translation. The French is on AT IXa 62.] Let us also point out an addition on the next page, which would confirm our reading: where the Latin says of the faculty of sensory perception "*in me ipso non esse potest*" (AT VII 79), the French says "*ne peut être en moi en tant que je suis une chose qui pense* [cannot be in me insofar as I am merely a thinking thing]" (AT IXa 63/II.55 n. 1).

21. All the difficulty concerning the pineal gland—and the finest animal *spirits* that penetrate it—stems from the fact that it invincibly entails what Descartes cannot allow: a spatialization, at least punctual, of the mind. But there is, in this *point*, a *double* contradiction: that of the mind as extended, and that of extension as point . . . The gland is equally not a point but a veritable volume. However, it cannot be said that the soul is found *within* it (like a sailor). One must also read again, in *The Passions of the Soul*, the incredible theoretical contortions Descartes engages in to refine the body in the gland and in the "animal spirits" in order to *permix* the body and the mind. For the union is total, and this is why the body of the human being possesses an exceptional unity (already present in the *Rules*; see "*Dum Scribo*" in this volume). But this unity must as well be presented according to extension, that is, in some place. The gland is this improbable place, *unum quid* too. Actually, it occupies the position that Spinoza will confer to the unique divine substance (the union is rejected by Spinoza because its problem does not arise: it is in God, it is God), at the price of the negation of the divisibility of the corporeal substance (see *Ethics*, Part I, Prop. XV, scholium).

22. "Metaphysics as History of Being," in *The End of Philosophy*, ed. Joan Stambaugh (Chicago: University of Chicago Press, 2003), 28. Original German in *Nietzsche II, 1939–46* (*Gesamtausgabe* 6.2), 432.

23. Ibid., 29/GA 6.2, 432.

24. Ibid., 31/GA 6.2, 434. [*Ichheit* has been changed from I-ness to egoity to stay closer to Nancy's text.]

25. *Principles of Philosophy*, Part One, §9 (AT VIIIa 7/I.195).

26. See, e.g., the *Seventh Set of Objections with Replies* (AT VII 559–562/II. 382–383). We should also recall that the anoptical system of Descartes's *Discourse* is not specular. See "*Larvatus pro Deo*" in this volume.

27. See "*Mundus Est Fabula*" in this volume.

28. Let us add the sentences that follow, which are no less revealing with their odd appeal to religion: "And I cannot refrain from pointing out here that this doctrine of the divisibility of thinking substance seems to me exceedingly dangerous and entirely at variance with the Christian religion. For as long as anyone accepts it he will never be persuaded by the force of reasoning to acknowledge the real distinction between the human soul and the body."

29. No doubt Descartes will say that the body obfuscates the soul. But what can this be about (since I do not know anything about the soul outside of the body and am not even certain of its immortality) if not that this obfuscation is already inherent within the mind itself as finite mind, and that, for example, the mind *might* not be able to conceive that its own substance is in fact divisible, as we saw earlier?

30. An instability, which must of course be understood in relation to the analysis of the constitutive stability of the subject of metaphysics, as Philippe Lacoue-Labarthe deduces it from the Heideggerian *Gestell* in "Typography" (in *Typography: Mimesis, Philosophy, Politics* [Stanford: Stanford University Press, 1998])—in relation to the whole problematic of the *imprint* (which leads us back to "*Dum Scribo*" again).

31. [The translation has been modified to allow for Nancy's emphasis on the pronoun I. The phrase usually reads: "whenever it is put forward by me or conceived in my mind" (AT VII 25/II.17).]

32. Letter to Princess Elizabeth, June 28, 1643 (AT III 691–692/III.227).

33. Part Two, §2 (AT VIIIa 41/I.224). [The phrase does not appear in the English translation, which reads: "The mind is aware that these sensations do not come from itself alone" whereas the French reads: "*notre âme*, par une connaissance qui lui est naturelle, *juge que ces sentiments ne procèdent point d'elle seule*" (AT IXb, 64).]

34. See for example the way he evades the question at the end of the short section of the *Principles* mentioned earlier (Part Two, §2).

35. See note 30.

36. "I am aware that certain substances are commonly called 'incomplete.' But if the reason for calling them incomplete is that they are unable to exist on their own, then I confess I find it self-contradictory that they should be substances, that is, things which subsist on their own, and at the same time incomplete, that is, not possessing the power to subsist on their own" (AT VII 222/II.156–157).

37. This problematic is reciprocal: the soul must be—"in a certain sense"—united as such with the body, and the (*human*) body must be as body disposed toward the union. It must indeed offer, *within extension*, the substrate for the *unity* that is required both by the soul and by the union—

or the substrate of *the* absolute distinction of *ego*. The body must contract itself in the posture of a soul, a convulsion that is called "pineal gland," and that, as has been pointed out, provides the soul with its first passion, its first joy.

38. If we can be granted a whole range of related analyses, all rigorously convergent, that could be conducted throughout all the aspects of the union in Descartes's doctrine. No matter from what side it is taken (for example, if we follow the project of a medicine of the body and the mind as it is proposed in the sixth part of the *Discourse*, or, again, if we analyze the apparatus of the pineal gland), this doctrine always leads us back to the matrix schema that we are exhibiting here.

39. As Michel Foucault wanted in *The Order of Things: An Archaeology of Human Sciences* (New York: Random House, 1970).

40. "The mind is united in a real and substantial manner to the body . . . not by position or disposition . . . but by a true mode of union" (Letter to Regius, January 1642, [AT III 493/III.206]).

41. Hence, the union is one of the "common" or "primitive notions." See the Letter to Princess Elizabeth, May 21, 1943 (AT III 665/III.218).

42. Letter to Arnaud, July 29, 1648 (AT V 223/III.358).

43. Letter to Princess Elizabeth, June 28, 1643 (AT III 693/III.227).

44. Letter to Regius, January 1642 (AT III 493/III.206).

45. "Letter on 'Humanism,'" in *Pathmarks* (Cambridge: Cambridge University Press, 1998), 251.

46. [The expression "*à son corps défendant*" is normally translated as "against one's own will," but Nancy underlines the word *corps*, implying that what resists our full appurtenance to humanism is our body.]

47. In a note from August 22, 1938, published in "Findings, Ideas, Problems," *Standard Edition of the Complete Works of Sigmund Freud*, Volume XXIII (1937–1939): *Moses and Monotheism, An Outline of Psycho-Analysis* and Other Works, ed. and trans. J. Strachey (London: Hogarth Press, 1964), 23:300. The original is found in "Aufzeichnungen," *Gesammelte Werke*, Vol. 17: *Schriften aus dem Nachlass, 1892–1938*, ed. Anna Freud et al. (Frankfurt: Fischer, 1999), 152.

48. See *On the Soul*, Book II, Chapter 1, 412a1–b10.

49. This series of motifs refer to a large number of texts by Freud. Its main steps can be located especially throughout *Jokes and Their Relation to the Unconscious*, in *The Standard Edition of the Complete Psychological Works of Sigmund Freud*, ed. and trans. J. Strachey (London: Hogarth Press, 1960). About the extension of the psyche, see my *Psyché*, in *Première livraison* 16 (1978). [This short text is collected in *Demande. Littérature et philosophie*

(Paris: Galilée, 2015), 283 and translated by Emily McVarish in *The Birth to Presence* (Stanford: Stanford University Press, 1993), 393.]

50. "Art and Space," in *The Heidegger Reader*, ed. G. Figal (Bloomington: Indiana University Press, 2007), 307. German original in *Aus der Erfahrung des Denkens, 1910–1976 (Gesamtausgabe* 13), 206: "*Das Räumen erbringt das Freie, das Offene für ein Siedeln und Wohnen des Menschen.*" All things considered, it is more the problematic of spacing (associated with that of "areality") that would be crucial for Heidegger, and not that of a "saying-I" as it is exposed in §64 of *Sein und Zeit.* For if in this section the "saying-I" is characterized, in opposition to the Kantian "I think," as that which always refers back to the being-in-the-world of the I, the "saying-I" in the strict sense, however, is in the end left to the inauthenticity of its everyday utterance: "The they-self [*Man-selbst*, built on the model of *Ich-selbst*, myself, J.-L. N.] keeps on saying 'I' most loudly and most frequently because at bottom it *is not authentically* itself" (*Being and Time*, 369/H. 322). The genuine being-one's-self will be characterized as the one that does not say I at all, but is in silence the thrown being that it can properly be. This seems to me on the one hand to misunderstand the fact that the "everydayness" of saying-I indicates also the constitutive permanence of the enunciating within any statement, and on the other hand to silence that which, without being indeed discourse, nevertheless constitutes its *opening*, an opening within and through which *I* is indeed *properly thrown.*

51. Paul Valéry, "Mouth," in *Poems in the Rough*, in *The Collected Works of Paul Valéry*, Volume 2, ed. Jackson Matthews, trans. Hilary Corke (Princeton: Princeton University Press, 1969), 2:50.